Be The Greatest You!

By

Mister Williams

All Ball Out Publications

Be The Greatest You!

First Edition

Printed in the United States
ISBN: 979-8-9892914-0-3

DEDICATION

This book is dedicated to my mother, the strongest, most determined independent person I know. I want to thank you for the countless lessons, and all the times you listened when I just needed an ear to talk to. Thank you for encouraging me to pursue my ideas. Through watching you, I've learned that anything and everything is possible if you want it badly enough.

I want to also thank my grandmother for dropping all those gems on me. I just love the relationship we have, and highly appreciate the times we spend talking our talks about our walks in life. Shout out to my brothers, sister, cousins, and numerous nieces and nephews for being my inspiration—you all are what I do it for.

Special thanks to my editors at EditPros for their unlimited support in aiding me on this project. Let's look forward to building a legacy together, and let no one separate what we may create.

Also special thanks to my significant other for her participation in the making of *Be the Greatest You!*

Lastly I want to give a special dedication to my all, my reflection, my reason to be seasoned. To my son, you are my motivation, you're my everything, and it's because of you I will always have a cause and purpose; therefore, failure is never an option. So just like the Energizer bunny, I'm going to keep going and going. Love you, Free!

Ball Out Family

A NOTE FROM THE AUTHOR

Hello there!

Thank you so very much for the purchase of my book! Before you continue your exploration into the world of becoming "The Greatest You," I wanted to take a quick moment to explain the purpose of this book.

As I have become content and accept the man that I am growing to become, I couldn't help but reflect on how this change was only possible when the man I once was had gotten out of the way of the man that I am growing into.

I felt that I possess too much intelligence to participate in the destruction of my community through a tumultuous lifestyle and to offer more to my existence than a CDC number.

As this is my first work of art, I wanted it to be limitless. I wanted to place a set of wings on this material that will allow it to fly through as many cities, states, countries, and continents into the hands of as many souls as possible.

My goal is to simply expose the many ways our brains process our mental thinking capabilities, to in return make this world a better place for our children and grandchildren to grow up in.

It is for this reason that you may find a fancy word here and there along with some challenging sentence structures because it is my intentions and wishes that you learn something throughout this reading, one way or another.

So without further ado, let the exploration of "The Greatest You" begin!

TABLE OF CONTENTS

PREFACE

This book was inspired by the state of minds behind those who participate in unbefitting activities while possessing a super exceeding mentality. For those who seem to find themselves participating or living a lesser than deserved reality, complacent with their current situation while fully aware of their untapped potential to have that much more, achieve that much more, to be that much greater. To deny or deprive yourself of your born-given talent is a hindrance to humanity and your very own existence. Many of us know we have much more to offer, not only to family, society or the world for that matter, but also to self.

It is this mind state, one can find themselves stagnated and idled in life due to this indolent sense of comfort that rarely gets challenged and therefore becomes a subordinate contribution to their existence, which in itself is an abstract to what may or could be. Now, I am a firm believer and supporter of the natural progression of things, but I too feel that some transgression is necessary to reach progression at its fullest capability. While no one can truly tell another what they want in life, one always knows what one wants for self, even when they don't realize it. However, there's a small percentage amongst us that don't know what they want until (A) they see it, (B) you show it to them, or (C) you just plain out tell them what they want or need. What determines the haves and have nots is the difference between the non-achievers and those who are able to accomplish. Those who dream it to those who live it, the ones who can't seem to miss their target in life compared to those who see what they're reaching for and know what they want, but never obtain it. Just think about your current situation whether good, bad or indifferent, and ask yourself which side you are on.

Here's where self would have to be completely honest, because here's where the difference of mentalities becomes extremely salient. The difference in these mentalities is the say all and be all to your natural progress, but what if it required you to transgress? Could you do it? Would you do it? Would you be able to be honest with yourself, identify what's giving credence to your current esteem of self, and openly challenge it in order to reach your highest aptitude in this only gift of life you have to experience? See, it's not enough to just want it, you have to want for it. It's not enough to envision it, you must set vision for it. You must possess a tunnel-like vision that is sponsored by undeniable determination. But what if you were selling yourself short with a limited vision from the start? Then the question becomes, "where is the state of mind behind the visionary and his or her restricted and to a certain extent, marginalized thought process?" I mean, at the end of the day it's just thoughts, right? Or is it your thought process, perhaps? So if that last statement were true, then why haven't you reached your goals? What makes your dreams seem so far-fetched and unattainable? Or why does that person of interest you keep sneaking peeks at, who you so desire to be with, seem so ultimately unapproachable? The answer would have to be the fact that it's all attached to your present situation and current state of mind.

Who you are and what you become, create, or contribute to society, the generation after you or the legacy of your ancestry before you, all stem from your overall mentality. However many of us fail to realize how much the world in its entirety plays on the overall decisions and choices we make in life. Life is based around circumstances and situations and the decisions or choices we choose to make in them. From that comes the reaction from the action decided upon and the outcome that becomes your now current reality but which started from that initial decision you chose to make or the choice you decided upon. Be that as it may, it's all contributed to your current state of mind, and the way you process the thoughts that cross it.

Ultimately we find ourselves settling and accepting whatever terms define the condition of our current reality because comfort is found there. Most would accept this condition solely based on the comfort found in it but the true happiness from the freedom one would obtain is then the sacrifice. In this book, I aim to target those unforeseen seeds that plant undesired thoughts that enable you to evolve from who you are to who you're meant to be. I plan to open up the realization of how much our geographical surroundings affect our comprehensive attainment. To explore the ideas leading to all possibilities of your unlimited mental capacity for what you desire. To challenge the mental restraints hindering and bounding you to a subordinate way of thinking or channeling your thoughts. After all, it is your life, so why not live it? It's a true gift that we get to experience only once, so why limit it? There is no one you could expect to reach for what you aspire for but you. You can be only you and no one else, so why not reach deep down within to become who and what you were ultimately meant to become?

Let me ask you a somewhat rhetorical question: Have you ever owned a device such as a computer, tablet or cellular phone? I'm sure the answer is "yes" for at least one if not all three devices. Now do you recall that message that just seems to pop up on your desktop computer or laptop that says, "A new version of this software is available for download? Would you like to download it now?" How many times have you actually downloaded that update your device rather than just plain out completely ignored the notification? Well, what happens when you continuously ignore that message? Your device will eventually start to slow down and it doesn't run as effectively and efficiently as you would want it to nor as it's intended to. The point is this: In the case of anti-virus software in today's advanced technological world, it is updating on its own without you having to do anything. So the primary intent becomes to avoid viruses and keep your device running as it should for the duration of its life span. If our world is advancing as technology advances, wouldn't it be right for you to advance as well? Well, maybe we too as humans need to reboot and it's within this book you'll find the means to upgrade your current thought process.

You should applaud yourself right now for purchasing this book and even taking the initiative toward investing in bettering yourself. The information you're going to pick up here includes rare gems that remain rare because not everyone is going to access the information from this book as you will. Right now I'll even go as far as to say this: I'm confident that after each and every chapter you read, your brain will change and shift toward challenging you to become the greatest *you,* and I must admit I find that amazing but it's up to you to challenge yourself in reaching higher expectations. My hopes are that, before the end of this book, I can help someone if not everyone, acknowledge the boundaries around an insufficient mentality with the intentions on encouraging you to Be The Greatest You. Enjoy!

Introduction

We have to start normalizing greatness within ourselves for the next generation to achieve greatness. Intelligence rules the world and ignorance carries the burden. The first thing that wise people must do is to remove themselves as far away from ignorance as they can. This journey of becoming the greatest you isn't going to be an easy one. It comes with a lot of commitment, soul searching and re-evaluating in the things that you believe about yourself, those things that you have been telling yourself for years.

Every generation meets their needs by utilizing the necessary tools and innovating creations of the current era as to adhere to their contribution toward bettering their conditions. These discoveries not only benefit themselves, but also reward those behind them. Whether it is the discovery of creating fire, the wheel, telephones, electricity, automobiles, airplanes, television to computers, our world as we know it is in constant change. These creations represent the innovations of mankind and a paradigm shift of the world. If you look at where we were, in comparison to where we are, you can imagine where we're going. So if the world you live in is in constant change and this change is in the design toward developing a greater world for you, then wouldn't it be wise and in your best interest to seek, obtain, and display the greatness within yourself for the bettering of the world, and more importantly, for the betterment of your children or your children's children?

You see we now live in a world where it's not enough to know what you know. In addition to that, you don't really know what you don't know until the time comes when the lack of your knowledge, education, or intelligence prohibits you from accomplishing and obtaining what it is in this one gift of life you were created to contribute. I'm going to use as an analogy something I learned from a child that stuck in my memory. I once had iguanas as pets. The guy who sold them to me told me that if I don't change the cage and make their living space bigger they won't grow any larger—they will grow to only the size their living space allows. Now as an adult I'm looking at it like this: if you place someone in an environment and that environment is limited in options, education, resources, and information, then that or those individuals will be able grow no bigger than what their environments provide.

Anything that is outside your knowledge you're going to lack perception about—you'll be uniformed and unaware. This is what makes it difficult for people with limited knowledge to function, especially in a world that's constantly advancing at such a rapid rate. Since we are all now living in the technology driven info era where knowledge is easily obtainable, that couldn't pass as a valid excuse these days. Knowledge is key and we now have more access to information than any other people in any other point in time. But it's not so much about knowledge of information as it is about where this information is coming from and if this newfound understanding is actually in your best interest or not. The source from which you receive this knowledge is important. We are still being misled, manipulated, and deceived living life walking with our eyes wide shut, controlled by influences and popular belief.

You have to look at the community and the environment that you are in and understand that the knowledge you receive is due to your education, experience, and what you are exposed to. Everything that you see, feel and hear becomes you. If you could customize your education, experience, and what you are exposed to then you wouldn't only be sustaining new knowledge but additionally you'll be awarded valuable knowledge that you can apply toward designing the person you would actually want to be and attaining the life you actually deserve. When you expand your environment you will expand your exposure.

If you're not surrounded by success how can you know what success looks like? If you are not informed of wealth how can you know how to obtain it? If you have never experienced love how would you recognize the feeling? If what you lack has never been revealed then how can you generate, procreate, or manifest it to your reality?

There's a difference between an alchemist (someone who creates or transforms things for the better) and manifestos (declarations of someone who proclaims their policies and objectives). Some people can drop a thought, draw it into their universe, and attract the necessary needs to them while others work with what they have to produce it regardless of where they are in life. You have to understand the significant difference and ask yourself are you a generator or a manifesto? Are you in tune with the design of your mind? Do you follow the blueprint to success as it pertains to your God-given abilities, likes and, desires as it appeals toward your personal talent, capabilities, and mindset?

It's a well-known fact that negative thoughts create negative actions. If you cannot fall in love with yourself who can you expect to fall in love with you? If you don't tell yourself that you are the greatest who can you expect to tell you? If you are unaware and don't possess the mindset to tap into your undivided potential then you'll ultimately lack the skill set to attribute to the many possibilities that you can and should achieve.

You must set aside reassuring times throughout the day for yourself to reaffirm that you are the captain of your ship and the master of your fate. Making a change to or in your life calls for you to take a stance, and taking a stance calls for bravery—and being brave isn't supposed to be easy. As you read along, each and every chapter is individually designed to appeal to the various makings of what determines the person you are and challenges you to become the greater version of yourself. Are you willing to sacrifice at this moment who you are, for who you would become? Let's become the version of yourself that takes full advantage of your potential.

Efficiency was predictability.
Predictability was weakness.

"Death is more universal than life;
everyone dies but not everyone lives."
—Andrew Sachs

CHAPTER 1

Having Full Knowledge and Understanding of Self

"You are a spiritual being that happens to be in a physical body."
—Pierre Teilhard de Chardin

Have you ever pondered over the meaning of life, your very own existence or your purpose for living, perhaps? Have you ever found yourself asking that famous question "Why am I here?" Since being the greatest you is what we are focusing on here, one must come to the understanding of who they are to further understand who they aren't. I wanted to start here because I like to think that as I have, others have asked that very same question, and I didn't want you to feel alone. Many of us think about what the meaning in life is, but have yet taken the time to figure out what gives their life meaning. What gives your life purpose? If you take the time out to reflect on the most significant events in your life it will reveal to you a lot of what you care about, what's most important to you, and how you should be spending your time in order to live your most meaningful life. Being able to identify this can have a huge impact on your happiness, productivity, and most importantly your health. Getting to know yourself can be challenging. It requires effort, courage, and honesty but it is hidden within your everyday attitude, energy, activities, and tendencies. Some of these characteristics you may already be aware of, while others you may need to discover.

How do we come to know ourselves and our fullest potential? One of many ways to know yourself is to understand that you don't really know yourself yet. Take the time out to analyze yourself the same way you would the outside world, co-workers, intimate partners, and even friends. This in itself is challenging because in order to do so successfully one must reach complete humility. Humility in a sense of recognizing your own ignorance in the sense of acknowledging what you do and don't know. The flip side of this, and the part which I find most interesting, is if you're ignorant to who you are then you're also ignorant to who you aren't and to your full potential. Take the time out to ask yourself "what have I avoided or what am I afraid of?"

Eighty percent of the world's population are unhappy with their lives, driven by the mighty mantra "I got to do what I got to do" or "It just is what it is" or even "Man, something got to give, shit got to change." Now honestly speaking, how many of you all done said those words to yourselves? Well I'm going to be honest and tell you like this: dude, I know, child's mother told him "Shit don't got to change" and it won't change unless you change it. The remaining 20% understand their life's purpose because they understand (A) who they are, (B) what it is that they do or did, (C) who they do or did it for, (D) what people want versus need, and (E) how that person they do or did it for changed or transformed as the result. The key to knowing yourself is knowing, understanding, and accepting that you are your own worst enemy and that you stand in your own way. The key to understanding who you are is understanding who you are not, the vices, attractions, and distractions you entertain that stagnate your very own growth and prevent you from achieving that particular goal or accomplishing and completing whatever task is at hand.

This brings me to the topic of self-examination and the ability for individuals to be able to examine themselves wholeheartedly without being biased. When I speak about this form of self-

2

examining I don't want you to get it confused with getting in touch with your feelings, delving into your unconscious mind, or finding your true self. It's more about working to form an analytical, factual, and defensible view about how to live your best kind of life. For instance, if you are into dancing, the collection of antiques, want to fight against some form of injustice, or even become a supporter of the law and fight for justice, if such things are important to you, you should be able to say why they have importance rather than just insisting that they are. This also applies to the contrary: if you see something or someone doing something inappropriate you should be able to explain to a fellow observer why they should not be doing so and why such behavior can be deemed unfitting. The only way to reach this level of confidence is by examining your own self with complete honesty. I heard a famous quote that says, "An unexamined life is a life not worth living." I feel it helps in appreciating others' viewpoint but more importantly it inspires you to hold on to your most firmly held beliefs, passions, and who or what you're destined to become in life, and contribute to your family and even society.

Take the time out to look in the mirror. Yeah, step outside of yourself and in this outer body experience turn around and ask yourself "who am I? What am I? Where am I?" Even ask yourself "how am I?" Participating in this inner body out-of-body reflection will help you understand what is going on inside and how that inside is affecting your outside. While we're here, pay attention to what's going on outside and how your outside is affecting your inside and you'll see it goes hand in hand. See, you must first understand what is inside and what is outside. If you do not understand what is inside or outside then you'll aim improvements to all the wrong places. Look at it like this: say you have a fruit tree, whether it be an apple, orange, or lemon, any tree that grows fruit. It's the roots of that tree that absorbs the particular nutrients necessary to feed into the tree what's needed to, in return, bear the fruit you love to eat. The roots in this example are equivalent to your inner body, the tree is equivalent to your outer body, and the fruit it bears is equivalent to what accumulates—your wealth. Your inner body is much like that fruit tree, and the roots that feed your outer body are the nutrients required to bear the fruit to your goals, and for you to attain a successful, fruitful life.

Self-knowledge and having an understanding of self requires a deep reflective self-assessment. It's about you coming to know who you are, whether that is through self-analysis or knowing yourself based on how you are viewed by others. Once a full evaluation on or of your self-examination has arrived, the realization of your likes, purpose, and aspirations should appear as clear as a sunny day and so vivid that you can see it, speak it, touch it, but even better, create it. Light destroys darkness as sure as knowledge destroys ignorance. So if you admit to yourself what you are ignorant about, then that part of you becomes covered up and once you gain the knowledge you lack or seek and remove yourself from those ignorant ways your pure self-shines forward. In the actions that you participate in, the ignorance of your unconscious mind will have your conscious mind believing that's your true and authentic self. The new self would appear upon ignorance being destroyed, although it was always there in the first place. Your knowledge that rises on the experience of reality immediately destroys the ignorant perception, creating growth as a result.

It amazes me how someone can tell you everything about a religion, God and how to get to him, a favorite sports team and their players, a designer's fashion wear and all of their products, but couldn't tell you a damn thing about themselves. If they were simply asked "Who are you?" they would draw a blank. This kind of a very knowledgeable ignorance is dangerous. This mentality we can attribute to a variety of mental deficiencies but they're neither here or there so I wish not to dive into that but instead only address the ones that complement my point, which is accumulation. What one accumulates can be theirs but not them. Again what you accumulate can be yours to possess, but it cannot be you. So your body is an accumulation. What you call your mind is an accumulation depending on what you are exposed to throughout your life. So let's look at the body: it's a pile of foods, whether healthy or junk foods. Your mind is a pile of impressions again whether healthy or junk impressions. Between these two piles, where are you?

Let me go on the record here and state that any impression is generic. What I come to realize with impressions is that just because I handle a particular situation a certain way doesn't mean you'll handle it the same and you shouldn't be compelled to think or do so. Or just because you were able to find success one way through a specific entity doesn't mean I'll find success in the same, which brings us back to the importance of one's examination of self internally and externally, inward and outward. Let's ask ourselves what is inward and what is outward? Well, everything is outward right now. The world is outside, the body is external material, all the material in the mind is also external—so what's internal, this inward that I'm talking about? Well, we know and can agree that we have a body and although some choose not to use it we can say we have a mind as well as other organs such as a heart, lungs, liver, and kidneys, but the rest is just belief. Not to question whether it's true or false

5

(We're not go waste any time in that department) if it's not yet in your experience. If you talk about something that is not yet in your experience you're lying to yourself and to whomever you're sharing this tale with. If you are talking about or sharing something you haven't experienced then it is mere hearsay.

Your body to some extent is within your experience and your mind to a certain extent is within your experience; the rest you don't know but we can reason. While the question remains, what is inward? True, you can walk in or out of a building, or in and out of a car—hell, you can even step in and out of a relationship, but how do you look or step within or out of yourself? Let's try it like this: all things that aren't you, you set it aside. It may be real precious to you like that expensive designer wardrobe—is that you? No, so let's set it aside. The beauty of your European automobile—is it you? No, so set it aside. Or even that wonderful house you just purchased—is it you? Not at all, so set it aside as well. Your avatar of a body—is that you? No. Your significant other—are they you? No. Your closest friends or even your children, are they you? No. All these thoughts feelings and emotions—are they you? No, so set them all aside. Now I'm not saying ignore your friends or neglect your children or material possessions, but everything that is not you set it aside, just mentally place it all in one big pile. As you continue to do this day in and day out you'll find that everything not of you will be placed aside and all that is, will remain with you. Once you have succeeded with this method, all that is not of you will be placed aside, the clutter will then fade away, giving you clear sight of your true self.

We as travelers of this Earth have too many ideas about things we have not seen. To many ideas about impressions we have yet to experience and this, my extended family, is a big problem. What I'm saying is that if you go by present perception you'll get all the wrong conclusions. Don't be in a rush to make a conclusion; take a step back look at it from a different angle but pay a little bit more attention. Since you're of this world and exist amongst the rest of us, your life is worthwhile and you will be doing yourself a disservice—not only to you but to all of mankind—if you prevent the whole, full, true you from blossoming and spreading the pollen from the flower of your God-given individualism to rest of us.

Try to think of your mind as a navigational system and feel as though you are in the driver's seat according to your conscious. If you do not attempt to familiarize yourself with this navigational system and how it works, where it's trying to go, and how to override it when it sends you in the wrong direction you will risk traveling the world with no purpose, ending up somewhere uninteresting at its best and disastrous at its worst. To explore yourself from the inside, envision a complete understanding of this sort of internal navigation system from the top down. This may get a little tricky so reread this if need be, but your goal should be to become conscious of the thoughts that press upward from the unconscious. There is a constant interaction between the unconscious and conscious principality of the psyche, which combine to create our complete personality. Most of this, however, develops and exists in an unconscious realm beneath our immediate awareness and control. Consequently a significant portion of who you really are, what you really like, what you are fully capable of, and the reason you do the things you do resides in a principle you don't actively understand or have access to. So in order to come into a more authentic and complete state of existence, you as an individual must attempt to make this part of the psyche conscious by tapping into it and combining it into the whole of your awareness. Once you've done this successfully you'll come to realize your individualism. To better understand this, it is important to understand the structure of the psyche which is designed by the dimensions of the consciousness, personal unconsciousness, and collective unconsciousness.

Consciousness is the principle of personal awareness through which one identifies specifically and knowingly with themselves. At the core of this lies another structure, the ego. The ego sits at the center of consciousness and provides a sense of personal difference, creating the story that people tell themselves about themselves in an attempt to maintain progression in their identity. The ego is expressed in the conscious realm as your persona, which is the outward effort of appearance that you as an individual actively display to the world. This persona, however, is often unconnected from an individual's true self as it often displays the character that one thinks or wants to be, according to what the ego deems as appropriate to a particular society and role, and not what is true to whom you as an individual actually are. In order to execute and maintain this suitable appearance and self-esteem, the ego filters various components of personal experience and individuality either into or away from the conscious principle. What it filters away and restricts, it sends down to the unconscious principle. Here is where we're going to separate the unconscious into two separate structures: personal unconscious and collective unconscious.

After the ego represses and disregards undesirable aspects of experiences and individualism, the personal unconscious stores and conceals these aspects, just beneath your normal awareness. They still however, continue to actively affect and interact back and forth with consciousness. The collective unconsciousness, however, differentiates from personal unconsciousness and other previous conceptions of the psyche that contain and facilitate worldly elements that are inherited through the sum total of human history. As a result of each generation of humans essentially imitating (at least to a certain degree) the behaviors of the previous generation, a chain of psychological imitation is formed, going all the way back to the beginning of human history. For example "I come from a long line of _____. My grandparent was a_____. My parents were some _____. Have you or anyone you know of ever said these words and can you or they fill in the blanks? Consequently, a reservoir of structures and memories is formed by this chain inherited by each human being. All these structures of the psyche work together ultimately to form what lies at the center—the combined, the self, the authentic totality of the conscious and unconscious. This self is who you actually are, what you actually desire, what you actually like, what you are actually capable of, and so on. Getting the ego and the persona as close to this as possible is the goal of individualization, knowledge of self, and ultimately a fulfilled life.

You may find that finding yourself, knowing yourself, and understanding yourself is one of the most fundamental ventures of your life. Don't follow the group mentality just because of its popularity. What you call universal values or what you all consider to be truth is just and always has been the personal expression of those or a particular individual that presented or promoted them. I believe that a fixed, puppet-mastered society code creates this group type of follow-the-pack like mentality. Just like a group of animals, a grouped mentality aims toward sameness, comfort and preservation of its occupiers. Similarly the moral code of society has been forged by individuals and then imposed on other people so that society can have control over you and human behavior. Although that can and may protect you from certain extreme behaviors, it also limits while hindering your individuality and creativity. Not only that but strict opinionated judgment of human behavior can even make some or most of you as an individual more rebellious, resulting in extreme antisocial attitudes and even worse actions.

If these controlled boundaries and rules become oppressive and unreasonably brutal, the rebellious response may be equally brutal. If the moral code of society is flexible enough then the people who have opposing views don't have to be extremely forceful to make the change that they want to see in the world. In real life, more often than not it's the case in point that morality is preached in a very strict and uncompromising way.

It's not only that societal, religious and educational structures present it that way. It's also the attitude of the majority of people that does not want to stand out from the group in fear of being rejected. Therefore every person that stands out "too much," according to the representatives of these groups, is someone who seems reckless, dangerous, and threatening. It is a well-known fact that people are afraid of the unknown and that is perfectly, systematically mirrored in this element. This is displayed and can be seen in our everyday life. Whether it's the Middle Ages or the modern day world this element is always present. Whether it was those who got killed for thinking outside the box, or at school when your classmates ridiculed you or some other student for being different and standing out, it's all cut from the same cloth.

The group consists of people who have amputated their creative dreams and goals and are feeling insecure and even threatened by everyone who displays those qualities. Those people are afraid of change, afraid of admitting to themselves

10

that some of their potential has not been fully realized. Although that realization is scary, individualistic people must not let themselves be dragged down by the mistakes that other people have made in life. Instead you need to go your own way, leave the group behind, and then shine a light so bright that it can't be ignored.

You can start by questioning and silencing those negative voices that you personalized when you were young. Whether it's a parent, a harsh teacher, a narcissistic partner, it doesn't matter. Whoever told you that you can't do things that you would want to probably told you that because they were afraid of your success, because it would expose everything that is bad about them. So they wanted to limit your individuality and pull you back into the group. Also being strong minded and courageous helps you withstand the frightening feeling of stepping out of your comfort zone, since it's an essential part of becoming who you really are.

Embrace the difficulty of self-discovery. No price is too high for the privilege of owning yourself. Your instinctive and intuitive reaction is to avoid all pain and suffering, the technology and the ease of achieving any and everything has made you ungrateful and you have forgotten that suffering is a fundamental part of life. However (according to philosophers) it's only when we are willing to face the challenges of life that we are spiritually growing. If you wish to be anything in this life, to maximize your potential, you need to take the difficult path, which often leads to isolation. When I say difficult I don't mean the hardest or the path most resistant. I mean the unpopular path—the path that intrigues your personal interest and or talents. Taking this approach is not easy but is one of the prices you must pay for the privilege of owning yourself. To keep yourself from being overwhelmed by the tribe, you must distance yourself from others, you need to strive to be free, and this might lead to severe difficulties in your life. You should refuse taking the easy path and you should decide to partake in the quest for gaining your freedom to be yourself, no matter how frightening it might be. To be free means also to be free from all physiological and psychological needs. In other words to not let them drive you but you drive them instead. For example, whenever you feel the emotional urge to do something like complaining to somebody, you must first try to become conscious of this impulse and then decide if you should act on it or not.

This fight is an inner fight, it's eternal. The struggle is to find yourself, and this quest is a much more difficult quest, requiring a much more different kind of sacrifice. For example if you were taught to be more confident in order to become popular and attract investors for your business, this approach teaches you to first analyze the primary root of your desire to become confident and usually you'll find that it's just the desire to impress other people such as loved ones, friends, someone you find attractive, or to prove a point about yourself to society in general. A simple analysis might make you give up this desire and focus more on what really matters in your life, on much deeper issues like self-discoveries. This endeavor can possibly isolate you and naturally make you a loner.

Refusal to agree to compromise yourself can very well put you in a conflict with many people. It means changing your lifestyle, it means giving up friendships and other types of relationships, to look deep into your fears to analyze your deepest emotions and to rise above them. You have to break down the chains of opinion and fear. I encourage you to challenge your own demons, but you should not cast them out as beyond them there is a deep meaning which you should try to understand. You need to get out there in the world, do things, experience different temptations but be always present with your entire consciousness and in the end emerge as an individual with a distinct strength of character and a much richer inner knowledge. If you do not go out and experience life firsthand in a fully aware state, you cannot claim you've lived your life. How far you can go depends how much you're willing to pay for that.

To reach the state of self-ownership and to avoid going through life in a meaningless way without direction, you must learn how to find your inner genius. To get in touch with your inner genius, you must walk a path you haven't walked before, understanding that you as an individual are unique and no one can walk that path on your behalf. Finding yourself is finding your uniqueness, that unique set of values and things you truly love and which represent you.

In all cases this sort of self-realization requires an effort of self-acceptance; and this sort of self-acceptance requires an effort of self-honesty. In order to actively move deeper into this psyche each opportunity you take to examine a personal feeling, thought, or action you must do so by accepting that often, you are not who you think or hope you are. Although self-acceptance and authenticity sounds obvious enough and appear simple, the act of actually working toward radical self-acceptance and individualization is of course far from simple and obvious. In an absolute sense, it's damn near impossible. To truly accept your weaknesses, downfalls, or unpopular interests to admit what you see, like, or dislike about someone or something may very well be inside you, but to confront what your mind has worked a lifetime to keep from itself is a task that will shake the very core of your psyche. Its demands a different kind of respect for the term self-analysis;, however, it is necessary for a fulfilled and complete life.

CHAPTER 2

Mastering Self-Control

"Educate your children to self-control, to the habit of holding passion and prejudice and evil tendencies subject to an upright and reasoning will, and you have done much to abolish misery from their future and crimes from society."

—Benjamin Franklin

Control is the power to influence or direct people's behavior or the course of events. I must say by definition that just sounds capital, doesn't it? Well let's look into the meaning of self-control, which is the ability to control oneself, in particular one's emotions and desires or the expression of them in one's behavior, especially in difficult situations. Now, you may feel a little different, but to me that just sounds a bit more gargantuan. It goes a little further than just control itself. For example, I'll use the memory of my childhood teacher whose name I won't mention. This particular individual had full control over us as students in his classroom, but failed to have control over himself while battling with vices and addictions to narcotics he couldn't shake to save his own health. Another example: since I spoke of him let me speak of myself. I would at one point in life give to others the best advice in the world, advice that would make a person feel comfortable with my wise suggestions of advice and that if not anything else, that I at least understood the difference between right and wrong. But what I wouldn't and couldn't do was follow my own advice to keep me from myself, which eventually led to finding myself being incarcerated multiple times. So I ask you, my extended family, see the difference now?

I'm going to go one step further and simply add, how can one say that they can righteously control someone else when they in fact can't even control themselves? The usefulness of the ability of self-control is that it helps one stay away from addictive behavior, or acting on impulse when it's better not to and it helps us to stay focused on the things that truly matter. When we make the distinction between the things in our control and what's not in our control the key becomes to strengthen the things in our control. A strong control of self ensures that you are less likely to be enslaved by outside forces that are not up to you. This means that impulses, temptations and triggers have less power over you, which strengthens your position in a world that's forever changing.

The control of self is one of the greatest things that I pray you are allowed to master and improve on each and every day of your life. With self-control it's not just about not doing the things that are wrong, but it's also encouraging yourself to do the things that are right. An individual is not mighty or powerful because of the ability to pin another to the ground. People who have strength, power and might are the ones who can control themselves at a moment of agitation, rather than letting anger and frustration take control of them. One of the great dangers and one of the things that leads a person into transgression, into wrongdoing, is that they become hostile and very reactionary. When somebody says something they have to react, and that reaction has to be harsher than the words that were said. Or they just have to have the last word and what they say has to be bigger and hit harder than what the person said before them. It might be that somebody sees somebody do something and they feel they need to top it, be better, buy more, or sell more. They need to have something bigger and better than others.

That lack of self-control, when a person is very impulsive, when they just do things and then worry later about the consequences, is a sign of immaturity, and it's one of the things that will cause parents to restrict the freedom of young persons and to exert more control over their decision making rather than allowing them a wider range of greater options and opportunities that an adult has. When you display signs that you can control yourself, when you become a person who takes things more seriously and hold things with greater clarity, you become a person who then has a greater standing in society and is given greater opportunities. It is in my wishes that you mature with your self-control, that you learn the techniques and the development of how to become a person who's in charge of themselves and not reacting to others or the situations that they are in. I want to help you become a person who others look up to and find value in you because you have a level of composure, a level of calm and a level of self-control that is pleasing and conforms to the ways of the world while retaining your personal individualism. Losing that control of self leaves you like a famished wolf with the desire to consume any and everything whether good or bad, and you worry about its consequences later. Focusing on your greater existence helps to protect you from that hunger and directs you to become a better person who is self-controlled.

I feel it's far easier for everyone to not have any self-control these days because of the efficiency at which we can get the things that we need in our lives. There just seem to be so many more temptations between advertisements and social media to persuade us to do something that we know isn't good or healthy for us in the long term. On the contrary, there are so many more opportunities for the average person in this world. Despite the creation of all these outlets of temptations, if you can learn to master your self-control you can stand out above others easily and use these temptations to your advantage. The basis of all self-control starts with your thoughts, but I guess any sort of success starts with your thoughts. So if you learn to gain power over your thoughts you can learn to control the flow of your life. The good news is all of our minds are very workable. As much as you feel you can't change who you are right now or maintain your amount of self-control you absolutely can through this ability the brain has to change through growth and reorganizing—it's called neuroplasticity. The one thought that makes this all a little ironic goes back to what we learned in the first chapter: you are not your thoughts.

Most people intentionally or unintentionally attach the idea of themselves to thoughts of what they don't have and what they think they deserve based on that little voice inside their head. That voice inside of your head basically governs you and tells you what you should or shouldn't do with your life, and having self-control is the ability to overpower that little voice. Think about when you're about to do something you know you shouldn't be doing, that little voice is coaching you on like, "You know you can do this" or "He's just so damn handsome and no one has to know" or "If I go about it like this I can get away" or "Damn, she's so gorgeous and well proportioned in all the right places, so I can't pass this up." Shortly after, you will become aroused and your body will start to follow and react uncontrollably to these thoughts. Then you start getting antsy or may become turned on by the thought of doing the do and it's like someone else grabs the will (wheel) over yourself and then you do it. Afterwards you snap out of it and ask yourself why the hell did I do that? What came over me? But you never really sit and grip the concept that all of this started initially because of that little voice.

Here's what you need to understand: you have the ability to become aware of these thoughts as soon as they arise. Realize that they aren't exactly you but society's programming, and overpower them. This is definitely not an easy task especially when you first start practicing, so let me explain this a little further here. The voice within you is a conditioned voice based on what you consumed over the years. Whoever or whatever you listen to over the years, not yourself, but over these past years since you've been born has shaped this voice into what it is—which further reinforces the fact that you are not your thoughts. You see, the reason why a lot of people don't have self-control these days is because what they decide to consume is a lot of negative energy that shapes that voice into being something negative. Whether that be what we put into our bodies, the news we're watching, the neighborhoods we come from, or what we're seeing on social media, that little voice may never be on your good side unless you take control of it. Once you understand this fully you'll realize you're actually limitless and what you can accomplish is limitless.

Try this for an exercise the next time you find yourself lowering to that lesser vibration or entertaining negative thoughts. Go into a slight meditation wherever you're at, wherever these irrational thoughts start to occur. Start to observe your thoughts instead of entertaining them, and do not identify with them. View that little voice in your head almost from a third party perspective. Look down upon that lower level of you, and as those thoughts arrive that try to overtake you negatively; simply separate yourself from them and tell yourself that this isn't you. This is just some freak conditioning from a world that's trying to keep you from reaching your full potential. Who you really are is a limitless being, someone who is capable of doing the work every single day to live a life of abundance. Continue to give yourself these positive affirmations until that negative voice vanishes, and then go back to what you were originally doing. It's important to try not to actively fight an uncontrollable urge to do the negative thing but instead to take a step back from what you were trying to do or not trying to do and instead immerse yourself in this little form of meditating. The key is learning to identify when this is happening, but like all things in life trying to master them is going to take consistent practice. Practice can never make you perfect but it can make you better. That negative voice can become less and less influential as you practice this, and you'll be able to control yourself better—but it will never go away forever. You know the saying, "You can take the man out the hood but can't take the hood out the man." That's why you'll need to practice this on a consistent level. Remember you are not your thoughts. You are the presence of awareness that perceives them.

If you learn to live virtuously then you'll live in agreement with nature and vice versa. Courage and moderation are just two of four virtues. Courage is a combination of ingredients such as confidence, endurance, cheerfulness, diligence, and high-mindedness. Moderation can be equally divided into modesty, decency, respectability, good discipline, and self-restraint. There are many ways to train self-control. It may sound a little dreadful but one is to restrict the usage of your smart phone, social media, and the internet altogether. I'm not saying go cold turkey and refrain from using these outlets; I'm just saying fall back a little and don't let it consume so much of your time. Self-control makes us familiar with the hardship that many fellow human beings go through on a day-to-day basis. Becoming more content with what you have and less dependent on what you think you need brings about a sense of peace and happiness.

Self-control is basically the problem that we have with all these desires for ourselves for the long term, but then in the short term we do all the different things. The fact is when we are faced with difficult decisions, between something that is immediate and unpleasant, versus something that is really good but lies in the unforeseen future, we often focus on the present and sacrifice the future. Let's look at it like this: imagine if I gave you a choice between half a box of chocolate-covered strawberries right now or a full box of chocolate-covered strawberries next week. Now if the half of box was right in front of you, would you have it in you to wait a week for the full box? Well interestingly enough, most people would say "Give me the half box, I'll take less now, rather than more later. Still not convinced, huh? Okay, let's look at it another way. Say you just hit the mega pick lottery for 100 million and they say you can have a portion of the winnings in one lump sum or you can have it all in small portions over a 30-year period. How many would request the large portion up front versus accepting small payments for the next 30 years? Now imagine I pushed this analogy to the future and said, "What would you rather have a half of box of chocolate covered strawberries in a year or a whole box of chocolate covered strawberries in a year and one week? Understand it's the same choice of asking if you'll be willing to wait a week for a half a box of chocolate-covered strawberries, but in this case both choices are in the future, so how many people would wait another week for that full box? Damn near everybody would, because in the future you are who you proclaim to be. You would be patient, there would be no procrastination, you would eat right and even take medication on time in the process. The problem is you never get to live in that future, you always live in the present, and in the present you are who you are and not yet who you proclaim to be. That's the problem with how we treat the present and future.

I think that one solution for a self-control problem in general is that to exercise doing something in the present you don't necessarily like to make sure you're not tempted in the future to do something unnecessarily bad. What do you think? Will you have enough insight, enough foresight, and enough self-control to do that? If faced with temptation with no tools to overcome it you're going to fail, much like many times before. But if you create something that allows you to bypass temptation in the way that I suggested before then maybe you can overcome or resist temptation. I'm going to use a personal experience to help get my point across. Prior to being released from prison I was in a halfway house, where I shared a dorm type of a room with four or five other men. It was a working dorm so we all got up at different times at the start of the day. One individual used to place his alarm clock in his personal closet across the room from his bed area. Every morning it went off, waking me up along with the other fellas as well. The alarm would sound until he got up and manually turned it off and this used to piss me off at 3:00 a.m. The others were used to it because they had been there a little longer than I had been, so it was just new to me. But he explained to me that it's hard for him to get up in the morning and that placing the alarm near his head would just tempt him to hit the alarm and go back to sleep, ultimately oversleeping and potentially being late and possibly fired. So if his alarm was in the closet it would force him to get up and out of the bed to shut it off. Since he was up and already on his feet, getting back in the bed would have been counterproductive, so from there he would start his work day. I understood clearly and it made perfect sense. Since I got up around an hour or so later, I started utilizing his alarm clock as my own and when it went off, I'd get up myself, fit a little workout in by doing some pushups and squats for that hour in between his time to wake up and mine. The point I'm trying to make is he found a method in doing something he didn't necessarily like in order to prevent him from being tempted to do something unnecessarily bad like going back to sleep and possibly getting fired, which for him would have been all bad.

Believe it or not there are secrets to mastering self-control, with one of them being habits. As easy as it sounds, forming good habits can be extremely tiring and demanding. You'll find that you're especially vulnerable to temptations within the first few attempts, but as you're consistent new habits would start to feel unconscious and automatic. Another such habit is daily monitoring. No matter what you're trying to accomplish monitoring your behavior is a great way to keep yourself on the right path. Think of it like a to-do list. Monitoring works the same way but instead of crossing things out, you're filling them in. This gives you the opportunity to see your progress happening. On the other hand if you're not making progress, monitoring will remind you of everything that you're doing wrong. It's easy to simply ignore bad habits—out of sight out of mind right? But when it's laid out on paper you can't pretend it didn't happen. Daily monitoring ensures that those mess-ups don't just slip through the cracks.

Now about managing anticipation, and finding it extremely hard not to buy the next big thing. How do you stop yourself from doing things you know you shouldn't? We struggle with vices like overspending because of something psychologists call anticipatory joy. When you see a commercial for the next-generation phone you'll get so excited about the limitless possibilities that you'll overlook one important thing—that it's just a phone. Anticipatory joy is a trick your brain plays on itself.

When you want something your brain doesn't always think rationally. The idea of improving your life stimulates the release of feel good hormones that reward anticipation and emotion but make it harder for you to think your decisions all the way through. Most of the time you're not excited about the things you want to buy, you're excited about the lifestyle that you imagine comes with it. I remember when I brought my first Mercedes-Benz and the joy that I felt at the thought of my peers' reaction when they see me in it, all the females I'll be able to attract, and how much of an upgrade to my lifestyle it's sure to bring. Well, I got a few ooh's and a couple ah's from my peers, nothing big really, while the women I came across gave me the impression they were intimidated by the look and they swore I was a pimp, and consequently my life didn't change much. After a week or two it just felt like another car. Although it was fully insured, I was extra cautious while driving it to avoid accidents because it was so expensive and I felt like a stiff monitoring my passengers all the time making sure they didn't slam the air compressed doors and nagged them to keep their feet on the floor mats. The cost of gas (Chevron 91 only) and general maintenance to keep it up was killing me, not to mention the extra attention I was getting from the police. Truthfully it was more of a burden than anything, and I was happier when I was driving my little Toyota. But I was in a lifestyle in which driving European automobiles was a status symbol. My little brother would always say "it's boring if it ain't foreign."

You see, if you allow your expectations to get the best of you, you'll end up jumping from one letdown to the next. Anticipatory joy actually isn't a bad thing; you're just aiming it the wrong way. Instead of getting excited about the material things you want, try to concentrate on the person you want to be. Start anticipating what your life will look like once you accomplish your goals. That way you're excited about something that actually makes you happy. How about patterned living? To master self-control you need to look at your habits a little differently. Let's say you're trying to be more productive. You might think there's nothing wrong with procrastinating one time. What I've come to learn is it's never just once. Whether you believe it or not, getting over today encourages you to get over tomorrow. You're rewarding your brain by breaking the rules. Imagine life like a row of dominoes—by knocking one down you're actually ruining the whole thing. The simple truth is that stronger patterns make stronger people.

Then you have calculated distractions. Self-control isn't about removing all distractions from your life; having no distractions can be as bad as having too many. Even though some distractions destroy productivity others can play an important role. They relieve stress and give you a chance to recharge. A distraction may even inspire or help you see things differently. Breaks and distractions build your self-control by enabling you to avoid frustration and fatigue. The tricky thing is that there is a right and wrong way to get distracted. Distractions are meant to be short and sweet. They shouldn't take up hours of your time or create more stress than they take away. The point is to give your mind a quick breather, not take it out the game entirely. A calculated distraction should bring you a short burst of happiness. Its main job is to improve your mood and refresh your mind. The point is to associate self-control with something that makes you feel better about yourself. When you do hit a rough patch this is an easy and effective way to get through without sacrificing progress you've made. Lastly there is productive forgiveness. I've spoken a lot about preventing mess-ups and avoiding temptations, but sometimes we just make bad decisions (trust me, I know all about it). You might skip a day on your workout, break your diet, return to a toxic relationship or slip back into old habits. What you do then is forgive yourself. One mistake can hurt your progress but it doesn't mean you can't bounce back. Without letting yourself off the hook you recognize your mistake, you forgive yourself, and then you get up and right back to pursuing the goal.

My overall point is we have a lot of temptations, lots of things around us, lots of fast food, and social media outlets. A lot of things that are aiming for our attention, time and money, even our food consumption. The amount of temptation around you is incredibly enormous. I came across an analysis that said about 70–80 years ago around 10% of human deaths were caused by bad decision-making like industrial accidents, job hazards, being hit by a car, and so on; now that figure has soared to about 50%, due to additional hazards, such as smoking, drug addiction, obesity, and senseless violence. We're just creating a lot of temptation and lots of ways for us to fail. A great quote that I heard someone say on YouTube which solidified that belief in my head was, "Leave your front and back door open. Allow your thoughts to come and go—just don't serve them tea." Once you become more and more in tune to your social programing and that higher level version of yourself, or the presence of awareness as it is also called, you will be able to overpower your thoughts or that lower level version of yourself almost all the time. Identify the negative feelings or thoughts as they arise, separate yourself from them and look from above them. Realize that's not you and that you're actually limitless, that you can overpower this and conquer it. Do what you aim to do or not do, not what it wants you to. That is the way you master this ego in which you contain what is trying to get your support and persuade you to participate in lower level activities because of what's so easy for you to do these days.

CHAPTER 3

Mastering Self-Discipline

"Everybody wants to go to heaven but nobody wants to die."

—Albert King

Okay, so here I'm going to talk about discipline and the mastering of discipline pertaining to self. As I was structuring the chapters of this book I admit I asked myself "wouldn't my readers feel that self-discipline and self-control are one in the same?" Well in hindsight the answer would be "yes," due to the fact that self-discipline is the synonym for self-control. But when I look up the word *discipline,* it has a meaning completely different from the word *control.* So then the answer would be "no" because since *discipline* has a different meaning from *control,* the meaning of *self-discipline* must be a different meaning from *self-control.* I then became compelled to do a little research on the word *discipline* itself and in its entirety, and I found the definition for the word *discipline* is the practice of training people to obey rules or a code of behavior; or punishment to correct disobedience. Then I said to myself, "okay, now how can I dissect this meaning into a person's own individuality, where it corrects self in behavioral deficiencies versus control?" Well, let's get into it.

The writer Samuel Thomas Davis asserted that "Self-discipline is about leaning into resistance. Taking action in spite of how you feel. It's living a life by design, not default, but more importantly it's acting in accordance with your thoughts, and not your feelings." So what I get from that is discipline is your ability to do what it is you aim to do, regardless of how you feel. You can see now how important self-discipline is outside of having self-control. It's building that baseline that's allowing you to act in accordance with your goals, whether they are long term or short term.

Why is self-discipline so important, may you ask? No matter what your goals are, you most certainly have to work in order to achieve them, and if you don't have any discipline you most likely won't put in the necessary work and you'll just procrastinate. Being able to delay gratification and short-term temptations is crucial if you want to be a successful person. Now it's a big difference in being disciplined and self-disciplined, and it's all about will power. For example, having a personal trainer can be much more effective for losing weight or creating that action figure body instead of working out by yourself. They might be able to correct you on some techniques you may be doing wrong and teach you some new ones as well. But the most important aspect is motivation and accountability. Being self-disciplined means that you will show up, do the work, and do it as you promised you would. It also means to have good habits and it's important for behavior change interventions because habitual behaviors are obtained automatically and because of that are likely to be maintained. You might notice that you are not self-disciplined. Well fortunately for you this is a skill. That means that you can learn and master it even if you're starting from ground level.

So with that being said allow me to cover some important strategies for building your self-discipline. Just follow me here because it's sort of a mind shift to what I previously discussed but goes hand in hand with self-improvement techniques that I too, previously discussed. Since we've spoken on individuality and we're already familiar with the term, focus on your own identity. To put it simply when you're trying to change your own behaviors forget about the goal you're trying to achieve and focus instead on the change in identity you want to obtain. For example, imagine two people trying to quit consuming alcohol and resisting a drink. When offered to have a shot the first person says "No thanks, I'm trying to quit." Now it sounds like a reasonable enough response, but this person still feels like a drinker who's trying to be something else. Such people are hoping that their behavior would change while carrying around the same beliefs. The second person refuses by saying, "Thanks, but no thanks, I don't drink." It's a small difference but the statement signals a shift in identity. Drinking was a part of the former life of such people but not their current one. They no longer identify as someone who drinks. The general idea here is once you embrace your identity you're going to find yourself acting in alignment with that change. Essentially we as humans feel this natural necessity to act consistently with our past decisions. Once we have made a decision we will encounter personal pressures to behave consistently with that decision. Those pressures then cause us to respond in ways that justify our earlier decision. Start thinking about behavior change in terms of the identity you want to personify from the goals you want to achieve.

Another strategy can be to frequently remind yourself of why you're trying to be disciplined in the first place. At the end of the day you have to have a strong "why" for your actions if you want to do them consistently. An anecdote about actor Jim Carrey helps illustrate this concept. After he had arrived in Hollywood as a impoverished actor he took out a napkin one day and wrote a check made out to himself for $10 million and postdated it for 10 years in the future. Then he put that check in his wallet so that every time he'd open his wallet he could see it and remind himself of why he was working so hard, and what he was working toward. Now this is something you might find useful as well. You can also find ways to embrace discomfort and embrace the resistance you feel toward doing something that takes hard work or that's unpleasant. Whenever your brain throws that "I don't feel like it" excuse, that is an activity to build that self-discipline muscle.

Maybe you can try targeting the fundamentals first—and by the fundamentals I mean the organic necessities of life like your sleep, your nutrition, or your exercise habits. These are all crucial to pay attention to because the part of your brain that handles executive functioning, the part that regulates your desires and impulses, requires a lot of energy and regular rest to function at high levels. You may even want to try meditation. Meditating has been shown scientifically to help people improve their levels of self-discipline. In fact, a 2013 study at Stanford University (where I was born by the way) showed that people who went through compassion training, which is a specific meditation program, were better able to regulate their emotions afterwards and this too is crucial for remaining disciplined. Also you can practice new habits. Building new habits is like a separate discipline in the overall pursuit of changing your behavior, but the initial stages of building a new habit often requires self-discipline because the behavior isn't automatic yet. So this can be a great way to not only establish a new habit but also become more disciplined in the process.

Essentially, self-discipline is the domination of willpower over basic desires. Being a disciplined person means doing things right when you are supposed to do them. It means keeping the promises you make and being committed to your true self.

A logical step is to remove everything that is keeping you away from doing what you are supposed to do. Our brain is built to avoid all kinds of struggle, pain, or strain. But don't wait for the right mood. Have you ever postponed something because you just didn't feel like it? Well, I have, and I'm sure I'm not alone here. Throughout the years we've trained our brain to be developed for instant gratification and not productivity, so you should never postpone anything to wait for the right moment; instead, tackle your task right away and then proceed to the next properly set achievable goal. Goal setting is a skill that will help you get things done faster. You have to be realistically ambitious when setting goals. A quote from a famous entrepreneur is "If you know the exact steps to reach your goal, the goals too small." Goal setting is most likely to improve task performance when the goals are specific and sufficiently challenging. So even if you don't actually achieve it you'll always be more productive. A good goal is an achievable goal that isn't too small; otherwise it will feel like you're wasting your potential. Also give your goal a deadline. A deadline would help you be more efficient and effective, especially if you make yourself accountable.

Think long term. Abraham Lincoln once said "The best way to predict the future is to create it." The only difference between successful people and unsuccessful people is that successful people take action. If they don't like something, they don't complain about it—they work to change it. So here is where you can ask yourself the following questions: What are you doing to improve your life right now? Based on your current daily actions what does your future look like 3 or 5 or 10 years from now? As soon as you imprint this in your mind you'll understand that everything you do today will have a massive influence on the person you become tomorrow.

Progressively build a productive routine and start small, because you won't change overnight. Big results take time to achieve, but with small consistent actions, you can achieve them. To get started on how you're going to improve your routine, start identifying areas you'll like to see change in. It may even help to make a list and group every single daily activity into positive, neutral, and negative activities. Positive activities are those that take you closer to your goals like doing research, studying, exercising, working, and so on. Negative activities are those that take you further from your goals like spending time with negative people, maintaining unhealthy behavior, and participating in toxic relationships. In contrast, neutral activities are things that waste your time and don't really have any impact on your goals such as being stuck in traffic, waiting for your ride, or mindlessly watching someone else's life on television or social media for that matter. As soon as you have your list you can go ahead and decide how you're going to change your routine. At this point you are supposed to eliminate all negative and neutral actions.

At the root of self-discipline is practice. Actually every habit, whether it be good or bad, is created through practice. Let's take your bad habits for instance. You give in to those harmful behaviors because you've practiced them. You've practiced checking your social media account instead of working. You've practiced ignoring your responsibilities and because you practiced these things, which you're very good at, and they require a lot of space in your mind. Your lack of discipline therefore shows a pattern of laziness and neglect. So how do we turn our bad habits around?

As bad habits are formed through practice so are the good ones. A disciplinary structure is a method for self-discipline and is built upon by order and consistency. Our lives are filled with chaos, and without discipline we're subject to that chaos. It's this chaos that drives you to slack off, to make poor choices, and to lose faith in yourself. In order to control that chaos you have to impose an orderly structure into your life. That structure will then control that chaos by giving you a sense of direction and purpose. Within a disciplinary system you practice healthier habits over and over again. No matter how disciplined you are, there will always be unconscious forces working against you. But order and structure could keep those forces from damaging your life. Of course, a disciplinary system affects more than just your day-to-day activities; it's also a recipe for long-term success. Every freedom you have that is for you is purchased at the price of freedom.

The center of bringing any dream into fruition is self-discipline, but remember your choices are always in the palms of your hands. If you want to build self-discipline, take control of your choices. If you want new goals or live a different lifestyle, it's your responsibility to make those changes. You have the power to create your own path in life. If you want to increase productivity you're going to have to make choices that promote efficiency, creativity, and concentration on your daily routine. But how do I empower myself to make positive choices, might you ask? Well, challenge yourself every day to make one unexpected decision. Eat something out of the ordinary, drive a different route to work, reorganize your morning routine. These unexpected changes are going to eventually remind you that you are in the driver's seat, that you and you alone are in control of your own choices. Once you realize how much power you have, you can use that power to change your life for the better.

Pay attention to emotional triggers. An emotional trigger is a feeling or a combination of feelings that cause a spontaneous reaction. Take a moment to think about when and where you struggle. To build self-discipline you need to recognize the impulses and pitfalls that develop your bad habits. Do you find yourself constantly overspending? Do you easily lose control whenever you get angry? Well, not being in control of your emotional triggers can very much cause you to overspend, to do things you may regret or to say something you didn't mean. Either way you're doing something that you don't want to be doing. What makes you feel guilt, shame, or regret? Where do your bad habits come from? To develop a plan of action these are questions to ask yourself on a regular basis, because it's important to recognize your emotional triggers before they impact your life. If you want to build self-discipline, start by finding your triggers. Think about recent moments in your life in which you lost control of your decisions. What do these moments have in common? If you look closely you'll notice one emotion that ties them all together.

Once you've identified your emotional triggers try to understand how those emotions interact with your behavior. For example, when you feel sad, do you get lost in thought or indulge in the abuse of a substance? Do you watch TV instead of doing your work? When you get angry do you tend to raise your voice? To identify the emotions behind the behavior try this as an exercise. Example: I feel sad, so I____. Or I get mad, so I____. Fill in the blanks in accordance with your own life situation and become aware off the triggers behind the emotional actions displayed by your behavior. This exercise is so simple that anyone can perform them yet have a powerful impact on your self-awareness. By acknowledging the areas in which you struggle, you understand where your bad habits are coming from.

You know what emotions are driving habits and how your emotional triggers affect your behaviors, but what are you going to do about it? How are you going to change? Using your emotional triggers and *I statements* from above, form something called a *then statement*— an example of which would sound like *if X happens then I will ___*. The goal of a then statement is to re-route your emotional trigger. Instead of attracting the same bad habits you're going to create a little detour every time those emotions try to creep into your life. So it will then sound like, *if or when I get angry, then I will take deep breaths instead of raising my voice like I usually do.* What this exercise does is re-route your emotions to a more positive and constructive action. Every time you get angry you'll know exactly what to do, and that gives you control over your emotional triggers.

Do you ever think about your goals and wonder, "how can I possibly do this?" Many people worry about how they will accomplish a goal without asking why. Before you pursue a challenge, ask yourself "why is this goal important to me? Why do I want to invest my time and effort into this opportunity?" The answers to these questions will help motivate you moving forward. Your *why* is the reason you do what you do. If you want to build self-discipline, you need to find your *why*. Why does this matter to you? Why do you want to create healthy or positive habits? Don't waste time worrying about how something will get done, for the old saying goes, "where there's a will, there's a way."

To build self-discipline, practice appreciating your progress. Every bit of progress counts, so keep track of your improvements. Recognize and reward yourself when you overcome obstacles that you've never overcome before. Not only does your progress show you how well you're doing, but also it's a great source of motivation pushing you toward a more disciplined lifestyle. Many people say they want to change, they want to build self-discipline, but they don't believe in themselves. They might say, "I can't stop myself" or just simply "I can't." These negative phrases will instantly destroy your willpower. Self-discipline and self-control do not exist unless you believe you have them. You need to have faith in your ability to overcome personal obstacles, resist temptation and make good decisions. If you are convinced you have no discipline of self, guess what? You're right, you have no self-discipline. But if you maintain a can-do attitude, you're capable of anything. Believe me when I say that believing in self is half the battle.

Self-criticism is the enemy of self-control. It's almost impossible to build self-discipline if you don't like, support, and empower yourself to succeed. If you're the kind of person who overly criticizes your mistakes, it's time to learn how to forgive. I'm not saying let yourself off the hook, I'm simply saying stop trying to re-write history. What's done is done, and no amount of regret is going to undo it. Instead try to forgive yourself and learn from your mistakes. Examine each failure as an important lesson instead of losses, and let those lessons influence your future success. It may take three maybe four tries before you find what you're looking for. You may even fail again after that, but each time you fail forgive yourself, otherwise you won't have the confidence or the courage to try it again.

CHAPTER 4

Mastering Self-Motivation

"It is not enough if you just live life as it comes to you like a floating leaf in a pond. Make use of the powers bestowed in you and soar like an eagle."

— Stephen Richards

Motivation is not some magical solution. It won't guarantee you that promotion at work and it won't stop you from failing at a task. A lot of people think a little motivation means success will fall into their lap but that isn't how it works. Motivation isn't the answer and it isn't the end point; it's where you start. Think of your goals like a road trip: finding motivation is like choosing where you want to go and why. Just because you pick the destination doesn't mean you'll always get there. You still have to put in the work by driving long hours and paying for gas. You'll still have setbacks like a blown tire or sitting in traffic, but if you pick the right destination for the right reasons you'll make it under any traffic condition or obstacle. Of course it won't be easy, and each obstacle will have you thinking about why you're even taking this trip in the first place, and at some point you may even feel like turning around or even think about giving up. You might get so tired that you settle for a closer or easier destination instead. This happens to so many people because they don't start of the right way. They don't think enough about where they are going. As a matter of fact most people just pick a random destination with no clue as to why they chose it. Even if somehow these people do make it, they quickly realize it isn't where they wanted to go and usually find themselves, where they don't want to be. So in this chapter I want to talk about motivation. I want to discuss motivating yourself the right way and tips you can use to help you follow a path toward your destination of lifelong success.

It's one thing to watch a motivational video and it's another thing for someone to constantly put a foot up your tail like your boss, mentor, life coach, or even your parents with every intention of giving you instructions or giving you drive, but it's another thing to be self-reliant and to be generating this motivation within yourself and at your own will. You might be reading this chapter right now and you might be looking to motivate yourself to do chores or some sort of side line activity in your life such as trouble with going the gym. Or maybe you have trouble with your health or figure that you want to get on track with the diet goals that you may have set out for yourself as a New Year's resolution. Maybe you're having trouble starting that report you need to finish, maybe you're having a hard time finding the motivation to complete the final copy before you reach the deadline. In addition to lack of motivation for those types of tasks, you also may experience a more pervasive lack of motivation that I feel honestly is a much more deeply rooted problem: the lack of direction in your life. When you feel like your whole life is just slow, your life feels like it just doesn't have much energy, like it's passionless and it feels like it isn't really going anywhere, almost equivalent to a ship in the middle of the ocean with no wind around, that's a lack of direction.

So these two types of lack of motivation are connected. We can't just draw a clear-cut line and say that certain activities are just chores and others are aligned within the direction of our life. Some of those tasks are related to tidiness and good hygiene while others are more arbitrary, but the point I'm trying to make to you is that if you are actually having problems getting motivated to do things in your life—like maybe you're having trouble getting to work on time, or maybe you're starting to notice that you just don't put as much effort into the work like you used to, or maybe you start to notice that you're falling off with your gym routine, or your diet just isn't where you'd like it to be—this may actually be a sign indicating that you have a larger problem. The larger problem here is that you might be doing a bunch of little things that you think are important, that you think are necessary and that you think you could not live without, that you couldn't imagine what your life would be like if you were to stop doing them, you think they're so important when in fact they're not.

This is a misalignment with your authentic self. Your authentic self wants one thing while your socially conditioned lower subconscious self wants to point you in another direction. Here's a great example of this: maybe you once had a dream of becoming an artist or a musician or some other pursuit that you're really passionate about, but you do it on the side because you have your 9-to-5, that real job that you do. Now if you're starting to lack motivation at your 9-to-5 job while your real passion remains music then you need to consider what's really going on here. The solution for you would not to be for you to receive a tip on how to get more engaged with your unpleasant disengaging 9-to-5 job. The ultimate solution—and I hope you can see this—is that you must take a look at what you're really passionate about. Since you're really passionate about your music, the problem is that's what you'd really rather be doing. So when you're at your 9-to-5 job you're so eager to get home and play around with your sound, do a little composition, and maybe interact with that fan base on social media that's been following you. That's what you're really excited about and everything else that you're doing is just a distraction from what you should be really doing, which is your music. But your life is so invaded, it's so complicated and screwed up as a result of government influence that the things that fit your passion, the things that are supposed to be your motivator to life, are buried deep beneath some surface. What you're left with is a bunch of activities that you think are important, that you think are holding your life together, but are really not as important. This here, right here at this point if you're able to identify it, should and can be a big transitioning juncture for you.

When you can make this shift, you then finally start to realize and realign your life so that the things that are at the bottom become the things that are at the top, and the things that are at the top become completely dissolved or just re-prioritized to the bottom. I'm going to go a bit deeper here but I wanted to get that out of the way. I felt it was important for me to state that because if you are a person who is struggling with motivation those can be very powerful signs for your highest self, and your higher self can be a very subtle influence in your life. What your highest self does is it tells you little whispers in your ears. It says a little whisper here; it says a little whisper there of what you should be doing. But that can easily get drowned out by the volume of the noise in your day-to-day activities. So you have to be conscious of that because we aren't looking for a quick fix by a multitude of implementations; we're are more so aiming for the root solutions, the root causes and then solving them permanently, not just placing a bandage on it for a quick temporary fix that's only going to arrive back into your life to bite you on the rear sooner or later.

Moving past that point though, let's talk about how you're going to motivate yourself and what it takes to really motivate

40

yourself. Truthfully, to motivate yourself you need to have a big enough goal. You need to have vision, and when I say vision what I mean is you have to want something and you need to literally have a picture in your mind of what you want. By definition that's what motivation is—it's the drive to want something. It's motive, which is motion and to get into motion you need to be moving toward a point, toward a destination. You don't just get into your car and drive around aimlessly, you're usually going somewhere, you usually have a destination in mind. Well, it's the same thing with your life as well as every sub-domain of your life.

So if we are talking about the motivation for losing weight or getting into shape, for example, well you need to have a picture of that. Yes, you need to picture what that view of you would look like, and that vision needs to be vivid. I know how easy it is because I have been guilty of devaluing picturing my goals for myself. I'll say something like, "Eh, I'll settle for just being fit." But that's a very vague image of what I really want and it's also not very ambitious or compelling. So your picture needs to be vivid, your picture needs to be specific, and your picture needs to be ambitious. By it being ambitious you'll feel like wow, how incredible would it be to accomplish that.

Now that you have you a vision the next thing that I want you to do is to put this into a larger context of your life. Too many times we can come up with a vision and we don't really see how it actually affects and ripples through our whole lives even into our future. Since we're projecting into the future, picture yourself. Picture yourself being fit and in shape. Picture yourself eating clean foods without having to place guilt. Picture yourself never having to worry about what you're eating anymore, picture yourself free from all the negative emotions. Don't just picture it but live into it as a moment and try to feel it and imagine to yourself what that would look like. Project it like year one into the future I plan to look like this, year two into the future I plan to look like that, then year 5 and 10 even up to 20 years into the future. What's your life going to look like if you actually put this into place, if you actually realize this, if you work your butt off and make it happen?

Then of course the flip side of that is to imagine what would happen if you don't picture your life, if you don't take action, if you don't pursue this goal and you fail to keep yourself motivated, what's going to happen to your health a year from now if you don't go to the gym? What's going to happen to your body five years from now if you don't follow through and clean up your diet? Picture that vision of a reality. What's going to happen to your performance at work? What's going to happen to your sex drive? What's going to happen to the relationships with your kids when you just don't have the energy to entertain them anymore? What's going to happen to your marriage? What's going to happen 20 years from now when you get hit with the news of some sort of diabetic diagnoses or signs of high cholesterol in your veins or heart disease? Project those things and make them vivid. It's sort of a twist that you play on yourself because you have to go into your own head and do this work. But it's good to go ahead and do this with the intentions of getting a good and powerful effect going. So dedicate maybe like 30 minutes to an hour to write out your vision, and maybe even picture it a little bit—draw out a stick figure, decide what you want, and just really think about it. Really get soaked into that vision, I mean really feel it and visualize it.

It's good to do that once but I guarantee you that's not going to be enough. To really motivate yourself you have to do something to reconnect with that vision on the continuous basis. I guarantee you that if you have done motivational exercises in other books or some self-help gurus has showed you this and they haven't been really working the way you want them to or the way it was promised may be due to this last point. It's that you're not reconnecting with that vision on the everyday basis.

First of all you must own your goals. Too many people, especially those fresh out of high school or college, fall into this trap. You might have an idea of how your life's going to play out but is it yours? Is it what you want or did someone else choose it for you? Growing up, around the age of middle school I had a neighbor who once wanted to become a scientist. His mother immediately locked in on the thought of her son becoming a great scientist. He got good grades and excelled in science so of course it seemed like a natural fit. Whenever anyone would ask, his mom would brag about how her son is going to be this great scientist in biology and naturally he started doing the same thing. After graduating from high school, we stayed in contact but he went off to a college with this great science program and started searching for potential schools for chemistry and biology. He thought he had his entire life planned out as he was so sure he had found the path to make him happy. But in reality he was trying to achieve his parents' definition of success. He adopted her goals as his own and he chose a good destination, but he never knew why he wanted to get there. Finally after years of reaching for someone else's dreams he sat down and thought about where his life was headed. It didn't take long for him to realize he was going the wrong way.

Once when I was in the 6th grade (or a little younger) the teacher came around class and asked all of the children what we wanted to be when we got older and why. Of course there were your typical firefighters, nurses, and professional sport super stars (we all wanted to be Michael Jordan, Jerry Rice, or Rickey Henderson) but my response to my teacher was that I wanted to become a doctor. My reason was that somewhere along my young life I fell under the impression that doctors, dentists and those in the medical field get paid the most money. Since doctors get paid the most money, what kind of doctor gets paid the most in their practice? So when the teacher asked me, my response was to become a brain surgeon. Why? Because they made the most money but truthfully, thinking back, I was just trying to top all the other kids' ideas. I knew damn well I didn't want to be a brain surgeon nor a doctor for that matter. Now the point I'm trying to make by telling you all this is that we are all surrounded by influences and expectations. Everyone around you will have this vision of who you are when really no one knows you better than you. Don't spend your life trying to live up to their expectations or run from their criticism. You shouldn't choose a path because people say you should. Your motivation has to come from you, it should stem from your talents, your interests, and passions. It should represent what actually makes you happy. I'm not telling you to ignore your family or friends, but you won't have the perseverance to achieve your goals if they aren't yours.

One trick to establishing motivation is setting aside some time each day to own your goals. During this time consider where they come from and remind yourself how and why you chose them. Not only will you feel more pride in who you are, but you'll also know you're heading in the right direction. When you imagine your future do you ever think about the little details? I don't mean that fantasy that people have about millions of dollars and living in this gigantic mansion with

Lamborghinis and Bentley trucks. There's nothing wrong about dreaming of being wealthy and famous but more often than not, these aren't actually goals, they're just things you covertly think about. You can't figure out a plan to get there because "there" doesn't really exist. This is what separates a goal from a dream. I often hear these terms used interchangeably but there is a difference. Dreams are flexible and easy, they capture imaginary feelings and actions. You might dream about flying, walking, or seeing through walls, but that doesn't mean you're going to do so. Some dreams inspire you to chase after something, but your goals actually do the chasing. Goals are concrete steps toward something you want; they have deadlines, cost, and obstacles. They can and should exist in real life, yet people don't treat them that way. They act like their goals are crazy and possible ideas so they seem imaginary but they don't have to stay that way. You can motivate yourself every day by visualizing your goals. Picture them down to the smallest detail. This is the same technique used by countless professional athletes before a major competition. They envision themselves winning and then do everything they can to bring that vision to life.

I once worked for an organization called "Teen Leaders of California" for which I used to sell candy in a van full of other kids. No one ever knew (at least I didn't think they ever noticed) but every time while en route to get dropped off in the areas we were working, I would take a second to close my eyes and picture my day. I'd think about how much I was going to sell and how I was going to sell it. I'd think about everything from rehearsing my script, my approach to the customers, how I'm going to talk to them, from my introduction down to the tone of my voice. I would think about my different responses to being rejected even up to the point of acceptance, and my response of being rejected

45

and simply walking away. This trick isn't limited to short-term goals; you can do the same thing with your future. Ask yourself as many questions as you can think of. How are you going to do it? How are you going to look while doing it? Who do you spend the majority of your time with? What kind of material possessions do you own? The questions you ask yourself may sound pointless but each one gives you direction and drive. You don't have to ask all the questions at once and you may not even know all the answers, but by forcing yourself to be specific you can turn those wild ideas into achievable goals.

I mentioned earlier how others' expectations can lead you down the wrong path. They can make you feel lost or unfulfilled by spending years doing something to avoid letting people down. But if you know where you're headed, expectations can also work wonders. After you decide on your goals tell someone about it. Explain to a close friend or family member where you're going and why. Express your vision and the steps you're taking to make it a reality. People tend to hide their dreams, some stash their goals on a secret "to do" list and others say they won't show anyone until it's 100% perfect (which it hardly ever is). Either way they're too embarrassed to show the world what they are passionate about, but hiding your goals may be holding you back. When you explain your goals you turn them into physical deadlines. If no one knows what you are doing you can always get away with not doing it. So you should create that expectation, and you need someone to expect you to finish when you say you will. Find someone who will check in on you and inquire about your progress, and make sure you find someone whose opinion matters to you—that way you won't want them to see you give up. It's important that you don't get carried away. This works only if you open up to one or two people, otherwise you can actually lose motivation. When you tell everyone who will listen, you may possibly in return assume an identity that isn't yours. Say for instance you're trying to write a song but you're having a hard time staying motivated, so you decide to tell a bunch of people about it. Those people will unconsciously think of you as a rapper or R&B singer and suddenly you've adopted this new title and reputation without actually doing anything. So why invest time and energy on something that you already have? This happens all the time through social media, in which people seem more interested in getting attention, likes and respect than accomplishing their actual goals. To make sure you don't fall into this trap tell only one person or maybe two people you care about and that way their expectations will fuel your success, rather than giving you an excuse to be lazy.

When I finally made up my mind to write books, I informed my mom that I had decided to do so. I was a little excited about the progress I had made so I called to let her hear how it was coming along. At the time she was in a car driving with her best friend while she had me on speaker as I read the Introduction to my autobiography. Now the bad thing about that is, she along with her friend would continuously ask me "How is the book coming along?" Ironically the good thing about that is she along with her friend would continuously ask me "how is the book coming along?" By them constantly asking me about my progress I now find myself focused on my project that much more to finish what I've started and I'm working diligently on the overall task of completing what I told them I was working on.

I wish I could tell you that you'll feel motivated all the time but I can't. Even if you master all the tips and tricks throughout this chapter you'll eventually feel lazy and unproductive at various times in your life. No matter how ambitious you are there's just no avoiding these moments of weakness. Most people would let this negativity stop them from pursuing their goals. They expect things to be smooth and easy but life obviously doesn't work that way. Every path you take will be filled with failure and frustration, but here's the thing: you know these obstacles are coming, even though you may not know what, when, why, or even how but it's going to happen eventually. Something will make you feel like giving up, so why not prepare yourself?

Another trick to staying motivated every day is to figure out ahead of time how to revive your motivation. Create a plan to navigate through your laziest moments. You may need to change up your routine to adapt to your life style. Once you have a clear definition on what you want, start your mornings by reminding yourself what that definition is. A good tool that is always highly recommended is a vision board. Use it to spread your definitions somewhere on the wall. You want this to be the first thing you see when you wake up in the mornings. Before you check your phone or take a shower you should already be absorbing your dreams. This strategy is designed to create accountability. If you see your dreams on a wall every day you have to acknowledge them. This immediately gives your day purpose and direction. In return you'll feel more driven to achieve. You'll notice after you build momentum that motivation works like a snowball rolling downhill. After you get it started it gets bigger and bigger as long as it has the momentum. To wake up feeling motivated you have to build that momentum by anticipating the next day. It's kind of like a Christmas Eve when you couldn't (as a child) wait to wake up in the morning to open up all your gifts—well, it's kind of the same effect. Along with spreading your definitions on that vision board you may want to add a short "to do" list. Before you go to bed at night ask yourself what do I absolutely have to have done the next day? If you notice your list is longer than preferred try to narrow it down to three or four top priorities. Keep them specific, brief and manageable. When you wake up in the mornings you should know exactly what's expected of you. You should understand what your goals are, why they're important to you, and how you're going to accomplish them. If you keep your list short and sweet you'll naturally feel confident, motivated, and ready to take on whatever task that awaits you.

CHAPTER 5

Having and Finding Your Purpose

"Life is never made unbearable by circumstances, but only by lack of meaning and purpose."
—*Viktor Frankl*

There are two types of people in this world: those who wake up in the morning like "yay, let's take on another day" and those who wake up like "rrrr," fussing at the alarm clock all grumpy and angry at life. Purpose gives us life; purpose is what gets us out of bed in the morning and without it we're just drifters, drifting through life with no direction, no destination or insight toward our journey, just along for the ride looking at life through eyes wide shut. It's there that your life can seem dull, mundane, or even pointless. Now by the American dream standards some would say just get through school, get a good job, follow your dreams, get married, raise a family, make a lot of money, retire at 60 to 70 years old, where it's now okay for you to start living and enjoying life.

The American dream—is that your purpose? Now these can all be good things that are a part of your purpose, but can't be your purpose because if these things don't work out for you, then what? And what if these things do work out for you, then what? Others would just try to avoid the whole thing and convince themselves that there's no such thing as a purpose and would try to replace the need of purpose with pleasures, excessiveness, and experiences. But we all know that gets old quickly, and as life goes on the questions arrive: what's the point of life? Why am I here? Or what does it all mean?

So what's your purpose and how do you break out of the anxiety in life? Well let's go over some suggestions. One would be to go out and help someone. Today, right now, go out and help your neighbor. Who's your neighbor might you ask? Anyone who is near you and who's suffering—the poor, the lonely, the sick, the stressed out, the sad, the broken, the beaten down, the depressed, the addicted, the lost, the hurting—basically humanity. That's right, the whole world and everyone in it because when we're living in this anxiety of life we're living totally for ourselves trapped in the junk within our own heads. Find or get involved with something that can help someone or everyone. If you were to find a passion to help, cure, solve, or dissolve people's problems your subject to find your passion in life and possibly get rich while you're at it—depending on which of society's many problems you solve—can turn from problem solving to purpose finding.

The next is to be open. The world needs you to be you and not some remake of what was before. It doesn't matter what someone else thinks. You take back your external focused control in which you worry about what other people think and you instead take on an internal focused point. You don't become insensitive, you become centered and you become powerful. Research even says that when you give up self-interested goals (on which most of us are focused most of the time) and you instead take on contributed goals, you function differently. Your outlook on life changes, your thought process changes, your learning accelerates, and you grow more.

The most important thing that you can discover is your purpose while existing on Earth. The process of discovering your purpose in life doesn't start or begin with your career. It's more so about your mental health and discovering who you are or who you are not. We were all born as individuals completely unique by our own design. The DNA that makes up who you are has never existed in all the years of the evolution of man populating this planet we call Earth. No one person walking this planet shares the exact same life experiences, growing pains, parental guidance, financial hardships, or other experiences in the same way as other people, so this in itself makes you an individual. Compare your birthright to a seed. If you water it properly, give it the required nutrients, attention and sunlight, if you cultivate your individualism, you'll discover your life's passions as well as purpose which, in turn, will lead to success. Money, power, and respect will come to you in abundance, yet if you don't pursue your passion to any degree, you're subject to incur the opposite, such as a life of suffering, dissatisfaction, and unhappiness. In life if you really want to have something, change something, or truly love something, then you'll find a way. But on the other hand if it's something you're not all that interested in or that doesn't have your utmost attention you will not be all that intrigued by it and would most likely not give it all you have.

I say you have to get to know yourself but even more, you have to fall in love with yourself. Then what you do while falling in love with self is investigate your individualism down to the finest details. You want to look for the little signs that reveal something essential. I do not mean to sound narcissistic, but I keep using myself as an example because I know myself better than I do others, hence I can correlate with my own experiences more than I can with others. As a child I would often talk to myself and while doing so I would make up these little stories. My stories would have characters, my characters would have personalities, and the personality of my characters would revolve around my imaginary creativity. So as I grew older, I couldn't help but notice my natural liking for a well-told story and, while incarcerated, my interest in reading expanded. Somewhere along my life I came across a magazine article containing an interview with the well-known and highly inspiring rapper, producer, actor, and filmmaker Ice Cube. In this interview Ice Cube was explaining how during a conversation with the late great legendary screenwriter, producer, film and television director John Singleton, Mr. Singleton had described how writing a film isn't far from writing a rap and that if you (Ice Cube) could write a rap then you can write a book and if you can write a book then you can write a movie. Now with my interest in rap I could compose a hot 16 or even a whole song but never really took rapping serious as I was involved with other activities. Then one day while lying on my bunk reading an urban novel I said to myself "Man, I can write one of these. It sounds too much like my life." But as I said that and pondered the thought, I mentally flashed back to the child that used to tell stories to himself, which turned on the lights of the author, writer and storyteller in me. The point I'm aiming at is what if I didn't wait well into adulthood to start executing my interest in storytelling in book writings and entertained my liking for that upon first notice as a child? Who knows but I like to think I would have been a lot further in life and definitely would have avoided those many years of incarceration. So with that being said I can recommend only that you dig inside of yourself and seek as a child those particular moments that will reveal some kind of excitement that you once had. The general idea is once it's discovered it will lead you to admit what you always wanted to be, whether a writer, teacher, musician, or an entrepreneur starting your own business. You're not going to be so constricted by tunnel vision or programmed to go into one particular career for one particular thing. Create a list of things you hate and things you love. Once you're finished, go over your list and ask yourself, "Is this because of what other people, social media, or the general society is telling me to hate or love, or does it come truly from within?"

You may overlook the fact that your purpose may possibly be right in front of you, which is to make the most of your present. Life is as you make it, precious yet unrepeatable; all we have is our past, and our present, and the future is unknown. Whatever has happened is our past and is one area in our life that we don't have a control over anymore. Let's focus on our *nows,* the present. The present is the most precious moment in our lives because it's in our hands now and we can define our future to a great extent by our current thoughts and actions. Our purpose should be to serve our present with virtue. In every phase of our life every waking day comes as an opportunity and it's defined by the time, space, and circumstances. I'll explain this a little further. Imagine you completing your studies for any particular trade, such as licensed barber, beautician or a doctor, for three to four years which is the time frame (just an example). But look at where you are performing your studies. Whether it's a trade school, beauty college, or prestigious university, this is your location or space and each space or location offers you academic facilities with many amenities, various comforts, and friendships with all the family support you would need—these would be considered your circumstances. But your purpose is right in front of you which is to make the most of your given opportunity and graduate. Your present will always provide you an opportunity to find your purpose. Ask yourself every time, "How can I make the most out of my present, my time, my space, and my circumstances?"

Your purpose is to add value. As individuals we are all

unique with different gifts, passions, and purposes, and we need to figure out how we can best share this gift with others because you get all you want in life only if and when you help others get what they want. Now, I don't want this to go over anyone's head so I'll go more in depth. Okay here's a simple analogy: say your high school is planning on a trip for the senior class at the end of the year to, let's say, Disneyland. In order for this trip to come into fruition the senior class must raise a certain amount of money by a certain time, and in order to reach that goal of a particular amount of money each student in the senior class must sell a certain amount of candy bars. You as a student and a participant will not get that trip to Disneyland if the school doesn't reach that quota. Or another quick example: say you're an employee, and in order for you to get what you want—which is to get paid at the end of the week—you must give your employers what they want, which is for you to show up every day on time and handle your duties and responsibilities as an employee. It's that simple but not limited to those circumstances. Shift your mentality from *me* to *we* and watch your career and life become shockingly successful. Be a creator of value. When you think of your certain circumstances there are going to be people who need you in some way or another. This may be but is not necessarily limited to your family, friends, or business partners you associate with daily. The truth is all of your most cherished dreams can become reality as long as you help enough of those around you accomplish their personal goals. The easiest way for you to understand the value you have to offer is by asking yourself these simple questions: (1) What is the one thing that comes very easy to me or what is the one thing that I am very good at that others can learn from me? (2) Who do you do it for? This could be your friends, family, or anyone you care for.

Family and friends will give you something to strive for even if it gets difficult for you. (3) What do people want or need? This will give you a clear idea on what's missing and would provide you the opportunity to fill it in. Afterwards give your best to each day's pursuit. Then go further because the more value you can create for others, the more value they can return to you. (4) Ask yourself if you are happy. You should always pursue what you love, follow your bliss, listen to your heart and intuition, and know that by doing so, success would have no choice but to follow. When you get stuck with doing something you don't love, when you are doing things that took you off your path for too long, you will forget who you really are, you forget that you have a choice and you do have the ability to shift your life in the right direction. Ask yourself this question: "What do I need or want to change about my current situation?" This could be anything like your job, your relationship with the people around you, anything in your immediate present. For example, if you do not like your current choice in any situation, then look to change it. Because if you do not like what you do, then you will not be able to add the value that is required and you won't find the success you're looking for.

Say yes to what gives you meaning. He who has a *why* can bear almost any *how*. Therefore, I propose that you say "yes" to whatever gives you meaning in your own life, the things that you find personal value in. In past ages and times the meaning of everything was assured by God. But as we are appearing to become an increasingly secular and scientific society, one can no longer turn to religion to find purpose and meaning. I find this concerning as the typical person would be driven to general indifference and unwillingness to find meaning in life, without help. I can offer three solutions that you as an individual can try to use to find meaning and purpose in your life. One is to utilize philosophy, art, music, literature, theater, or other parts of the humanities to provide similar benefits. The humanities offer you the ability to inspect your sufferings and your efforts, and a chance to see that your life is not so different from those around you. The humanities can offer insights on how you might tackle problems we all face. However it's important that you see them as a tool for living and not just an academic study. Reading history not just for the facts but for what those facts tells you. Seeing them as a way to educate yourself, or watching tragic plays to see and comprehend the beauty in sad events, not just the entertainment. My second option is to become someone who creates their own meaning, values, and purpose in life without reference to outside influences. Such an individual can overcome the problem of the meaning of life by simply inventing your own meaning and taking full responsibility for it. By history terms a few men took on this course of living such as Julius Caesar, Marcus Garvey, Charles "Lucky" Luciano, Malcolm X and Dr. Martin Luther King, just to name a few. We as humans can hope to find some meaning in looking inward and evaluating what things we really value and what things we only say we like because society tells us to.

I see the psychological evolution of humanity as an ever-advancing story and one in which you should take part. If you see no value in creating your purpose then I suggest another method to finding meaning, which is loving your life no matter what it has in it. The love of fate can be an interesting idea and one which can offer us a great deal of comfort when you most need it. To love your fate is to know that everything that has happened to you in your life, the good the bad, and indeed the ugly, has contributed to who you are and what you are doing at this very moment. Trying to create yourself will lead to some failures, embracing those failures alongside your successes can help re-spark the love and life and help you see the meaning of it even in the worse moments.

After you have figured out your life's purpose and what you want to do, you might not know how to go ahead or which road to take. You may even lack certain skills. So the best way to move forward is just by starting with what you want to do. If you want to be a writer, start by writing something every day. If you wish to be a rapper or R&B singer, start recording something every day. For anything you want to do you don't need inspiration, research, or advice for that matter. You just start practicing something you're interested in and tackle every day as it comes because it's your purpose that will give you internal desire, drive, and motivation that sets you in motion to move forward toward your goal.

Keep in mind that purpose is meaningless without self-control and self-discipline. Self-control and discipline are the fundamental actions, mindset and reasoning that keep you in a steady routine and making progress toward whatever you're pursuing. Even after having a solid purpose and a plan you need to show up every day and put in the necessary work. This simple act of showing up will definitely bring you closer to achieving whatever you want. Stop worrying about the outcome. You can only control the power over your mind, not outside events.

When we as humans set out to do something we often get overwhelmed by fear. We can tend to worry too much about the outcome. A big part of that worrying has to do with the *what if* factor, which we tend to contemplate in our minds. What if this happens? What if that happens? The fact of the matter is that your mind is very much like the camera lens on your cell phone you use for all those selfies; you'll get exactly what you're focused on. If you focus on problems you'll receive more problems. If you focus on something positive eventually you'll start receiving positive things and your life will steer in that direction. You need to stop worrying about the outcome and all the other things that are not in your control and concentrate on things that are in your control. If you want to be a successful professional athlete don't worry about the competition or opinions of others, but rather concentrate on what you control, such as your training, what you eat, and your progress. Just by concentrating on things you can control, you will be able to put yourself in the driver's seat and be able to give yourself control over your destination and perhaps your ETA (estimated time of arrival).

Since I mentioned the camera on your phone let me also mention that phone may very well be the reason why you haven't found your purpose. As humans we must understand that our brains are naturally wired to want more. One of the most basic elements for living a meaningful life full of purpose is plainly having a reason. We tend to try to have a purpose, but we often exist in ways that aren't fulfilling at all. I think this is because most people these days are too worried about and focused on what other people are doing. You can become so tuned in to social media that you care more about what's going on in someone else's life than in your own. Right here I'm going to share something that my 6th or 7th grade teacher Mr. Haggins said to us in class during one of his many rants. His words were, "My business is the best business and if you don't got no business of your own, make it your business to leave my business alone." But he shot that out so quick and swift, I raised my hand to ask him to say that again and it stuck with me for the rest of my life (shout out to you, Mr. Haggins, for your wisdom is much appreciated). Just think about it like this: Do you think humans 100 years ago were anxiously waiting on their favorite artist to drop another album or patiently waiting for the next episode of their favorite show only to be glued to the television monitor? I highly doubt it; they were most likely going about their lives and handling their business. Now I went a little extreme in that comparison but the point I'm trying to make here is, you got to have enough of you own life to live than watching or becoming so consumed in what's going on in someone else's, right? Once, during a conversation this young cat couldn't understand how I didn't know or keep up with a current affair in something related to either the NBA or the NFL and was trying to make a joke about it at my expense, so my response to him was "they're already situated, established and successful, with exotic cars and multi-million dollar homes. You can sit here and tell me everything about them, yet they don't even know you exist. Instead of worrying about their life and what's going on, I'm too busy working on a legacy of my own." I just couldn't resist the teachable moment but the expression on his face let me know that he had picked up what I was putting down and understood my point clearly. He spent the rest of that time around me picking my brain versus trying to stir up a joke about me.

This leads me to recommend reaching out to a good mentor or someone you most likely look up to as a role model. This person can be a friend, family member, or an associate who has already achieved the goals you're working toward. A positive role model could influence your actions and motivate you to strive to uncover your true potential and passions, and overcome any weaknesses you may or may not have. If you pick associates whose behavior is better than yours, you'll eventually drift in that direction. You know the saying "If you hang around nine millionaires you have action at becoming the 10th." Well, that's very much true. While doing this it's imperative that you ignore negative people. When you announce your purpose and set out to achieve your goals, you will attract some negativity from people around you and that's okay because that's life. There would always be people there to tell you that you can't do something, that you're not smart enough, you don't have enough resources or connections, you don't have enough money, and so on. But you have to ignore the negativity if you want to achieve your goals. Their voice does not deserve to be heard. Don't hand over your piece of mind to outsiders to do with as they please. Look at it like this: a person who brings you negativity is merely an obstruction, and an obstacle is just a way through. Just know that the obstacle to action advances action, and what stands in the way becomes the way. On your pursuit there's going to be obstacles for sure. You'll overcome some and others are going to be difficult to tackle. Life happens but in these circumstances it's not in your best interest to turn to your negative side and start concentrating on things you can't do anything about. Change your perception and realize that whatever happens or happened is not in your control and you can do nothing about your current situation but you can turn an obstacle into an opportunity by practicing virtue over things you do have control over, which is the life ahead of you.

Always know and keep in mind that there's never an end. Let me remind you that your worth is no greater than your ambitions. There will be a time when you find your purpose and will have achieved everything. There will be a time when you aren't sure where you want to go next. After you've reached your goals, always look for ways to evolve and expand your ambitions. If you feel stuck now that you have achieved everything, it might be a perfect time to try some new things and gain new experiences so that you have new things to work toward. Life will always provide you with an opportunity to find a new purpose and all it takes is going out there and doing everything righteously.

The only thing that I'm left to conclude is that you and I are designed to be purpose-seeking mechanisms. You've been shaped by life through good and bad experiences, and both the good experiences and the bad experiences are there to teach you something about you. If you look very carefully at those you can determine what your purpose is. Every person in this world can clarify the purpose of their life and in return be the key to every door and in return live their best life.

CHAPTER 6

Understanding of Self's Mental Mind State

"A wandering mind, is an unhappy mind."

—Matt Killingsworth

We all should give enough time and attention to our mental health and mental well-being. The healthier you are mentally, the better you are physically and psychologically. It seems that stress and being overwhelmed are so prevalent in today's society. Although stress itself isn't a mental health issue, it's often for many people a starting point. I often think that sometimes we get stuck in our heads and not in our bodies. Thinking isn't necessarily the solution to our problems. In fact, it may very well be the cause of the effect. I'll be the first to admit that I, like many people, can spend too much time overthinking. It has been proven that overthinking can lead to psychological stress. Well, the problem I had with that is I've always thought my way out of my problems. But on the contrary, I have also always thought my way into the majority of my problems, as well. So I wondered for quite some time, how can I balance my thinking and psychological well-being to enhance my state of mind?

First let's look at the mind for what the mind is. If you sit back and think about the English word "mind," it doesn't really say anything because it's just a word that doesn't actually describe the different dimensions of what the mind is. It would be described as one's intellect, but what is the mind and how does it actually work? During my research of this particular topic I've come to understand that there is no mind, there is just your physical body and your mental body. What you're calling or referring to as your mind is just a certain combination of memories, intelligence, and experiences. Everyone has memories, but few can remember what their eldest ancestor looked like; however, you share their features. Consciously you can't remember them, but your body does 100%. Whether your ancestors were 5, 10, or 15 generations ago, your body still remembers the DNA and genetic structure you share with them. It has not forgotten and will never forget. Now your mind on the other hand is not capable of this memory. Our bodies have a trillion times more memory than what we call our minds.

I'll follow up with this theory as we understand the context of thought. You can't think beyond the experiences that you have already gathered. That means if you dedicate yourself to your thought process, if you cherish your thought process, you're insuring nothing new will ever happen in your life. That's why when you think about it, your thoughts are never given much significance. What you think are your psychological issues, and they are yours alone. Your issues are important to you, and someone else's issues are important to them. Everyone thinks their issues are the most important issues in the world, because they are concerned with their own psychological issues at hand. But these particular issues that affect us right now are small compared to the whole life process, therefore they shouldn't determine the nature or direction of your life. Life itself is a much deeper intelligence than intellect.

Thinking back as child, I remember going outside, playing around and having fun with other children. In those days, we always had something to do. Even when there wasn't anything to do we created something, so being bored was little to nonexistent. When I look at kids today, it seems that without a gaming console or a smartphone in their hands they have very little to nothing to do, and the creativity level is slim to none. When you see kids at 5, 10, or 15 years of age looking bored, it is because they've seen and been exposed to so much in or about life through a phone screen. What we are experiencing today with all this technology is that we have too much information without the experience. The problem with that is if too much information is received without the experience, the cheerfulness in life will be gone and a false sense of knowing becomes strong. This is the danger of intellect, because intellectuals want to dissect everything. What I mean by that is intellect is like a knife, the sharper it is the better it is—it wants to dissect and know. Dissection works with some things but not with all aspects of life. Life could not be known by slicing and breaking it up. You can know physical things by breaking them up, but you cannot know life by breaking it into little pieces; however, this is the nature of the intellect.

The whole modern science has evolved from human intellect, and because people can now Google a question they think they are rocket scientists. Technology has brought much comfort and convenience, but it will not bring life to us. Intellect could be useful depending on what it's identified with. Whatever you identify with, your intellect will function solely around it. It's simple when you look at it like this, if you for instance say I'm a Christian or a Muslim, everything to you do whether it falls under the Christianity or Islamic belief system will look beautiful. If you say to yourself, "I'm going to be the greatest musician," everything related to the musical lifestyle looks appealing. So whatever it is you identify with, that's how your intellect will function.

Your brain is constantly changing and being shaped by forces around you that's out of your control. But at the same time, you are typically aware of what these forces are. Your brain is changing whether it being wittingly or unwittingly; however, most of the time it's unwittingly. Most of the time you're just not aware and possess no control over these outside influences. The work that I intend to further explain is that you can take more responsibility for your own brain by transforming your own mind. But first I'd like to share with you what some of the consequences are for having your brain shaped unknowingly. For instance, what you like is what you like. You don't have to believe, like, dress, or act a certain way because it's the norm, or because it's the fad, or it's what's in style, or what's in popular demand for that matter. You may want or like something completely different than what's in style, and that's ok.

Throughout life, while trying to figure out and balance the many varieties of obstacles that are thrown upon you, it's easy to become consumed by the influences you are exposed to and the influencers around you. In times like these it's imperative that you take the time out to find what's compatible to your mental liking and particular interests. All of this falls under the pretense of learning yourself, studying yourself, understanding yourself and, finally, knowing yourself. Now in order to be able to successfully achieve this understanding, you have to know how your brain works and how your brain sustains the learning process.

So how do we learn, and why does it seem like some of us learn things more easily than others? As I was researching this topic, those are the questions that fascinated me. Brain research, I've found, is one of the greatest boundaries and the understanding of human physiology (the branch of biology that deals with the functions of living organisms), while also taking into consideration what makes us who we are. What we currently know about our brains is breathtaking, but it's also changing at a rapid pace. Much about what you know or thought you knew and understood about your brain might actually turn out to be untrue or incomplete. Some of these misconceptions are more obvious than others. One misconception about our brain is that we only use parts of it at a time. Growing up I was told and always believed that we as humans only use 10% of our brain. I've come to learn that couldn't be further from the truth. Another misconception is that our brain is stagnant when we're doing nothing. This is also untrue. It turns out that even when you're resting and thinking of nothing your brain is highly active.

Every time you learn a new fact or skill you change your brain. Brain reorganization helps to support recovery after the brain has been damaged. The key to each of these changes from adolescence to adulthood to convalescence is a term called neuroplasticity, which is the ability of neural networks in the brain to change through growth and reorganization, addressed in chapter 2. Your brain can change in three very basic ways to support learning, with the first being chemical. So your brain actually functions by transferring chemical signals between brain cells called neurons, and these trigger a series of actions and reactions. To support learning, your brain can increase the amount or the concentration of the chemical signaling that's taking place between these neurons. Now because this change can happen very rapidly, it only supports short-term memory or short-term improvement in the performance of a motor skill.

The second way that the brain can change to support learning is by altering its structure. During the process of learning, the brain can change the connection between neurons. At this point the physical structure of the brain is actually changing so it takes a bit more time. These types of changes are related to long-term memory or the long-term improvement in a motor skill. I'll give

67

you an example as to how these processes interact: Say you're trying to learn a new motor skill, like playing an instrument or juggling for instance. You'll have the experience of getting better and better within a single session of practicing, and then you'll think to yourself "Okay, I got it." However, you return the next day and all those improvements from the day before are lost. You might find yourself asking, "What happened?" Well in the short-term, your brain was able to increase the chemical signaling between your neurons. But for some reason, those changes did not bring about the structural changes that are necessary to support the long-term memory. Keep in mind long-term memory takes time, and what you see in the short-term does not reflect learning. It's these physical changes that are now going to support long-term memories, and chemical changes that support short-term memories.

Structural changes can lead to integrated networks of brain regions that function together to support learning. They can also lead to certain brain regions that are important for very specific behaviors to change your structure or to enlarge it. Here are some examples of that: People who read Braille have larger hand sensory areas in their brain than those of us who don't. Your dominant hand movement region, which is on the left side of your brain if you're right handed, is larger than the other side. Studies have shown that London taxi cab drivers who actually have to memorize a map of London to get their taxi cab license have larger brain regions devoted to spatial or mapping memories.

Finally, the way that your brain can change to support learning is by altering its function. As you use the brain region it becomes more and more excitable and easy to recall, because the areas that increase your excitement shift how and when they are activated. With learning, the whole network of brain activity are shifting and changing. Neuroplasticity is supported by chemical, structural, and functional changes and these changes are happening throughout the whole brain. Together they support learning and they're taking place all the time.

So, we just discussed how incredible the brain is, but it may leave one asking: "Why can't I learn what I choose with ease?" "Why do my kids sometimes fail in school?" "Why as we get older do we tend to forget things?" or "Why don't people fully recover from brain damage after suffering a stroke?" What is it that limits or facilitates neuroplasticity? As it turns out the best operator to neuroplasticity change in your brain is your behavior. Your brain is being structured by everything that you either do or don't do. One thing to keep in mind and always remember is that there is no one-size-fits-all when it comes to the brain and its approach to learning. With that being said, it's no recipe for learning, and if there were one, the recipe would be to learn how you learn. Take the necessary time out to learn how your children learn. Naturally, when it comes to learning new things, some people will need a lot more practice than others. So the shaping of your brain is far too unique for there to be any single intervention that's going to work for everyone. This realization must force and encourage you to consider something called personalized medicine. This is the idea that each and every individual requires their own intervention (your own intervention).

Now on a brighter side of things—know that the unique structure and function of all of our brain behaviors that we employ in our everyday lives are very important. These behaviors are changing the way your brain functions. I believe you have to consider not just personalized medicine but personalized learning. This requires you to dig into yourself, learn about yourself, and know yourself. The uniqueness of your brain will affect you both as a learner and a teacher. This idea would help you to understand why some children can thrive in traditional education settings while others don't. Why is it that some of us can learn other languages easily and others can pick up any sport and excel at it effortlessly?

I'm going to focus on four challenges that have been critical in the society in which we all live today. These particular challenges are failures of our well-being in very important ways. The first is the state of distraction or being distracted. I've learned from a study that was conducted a few years ago that if we text people out and about in the world these three questions: (1) "What are you doing right now?" (2) "Where is your mind right now? Is it focused on what you're doing or is it focused elsewhere?" and (3) "At this very moment how happy or unhappy are you?" what their responses would be. Researchers found that average American adults spend 47% of their waking hours not paying attention to what they are actually doing. Also when they were not paying attention to what they were doing, they were significantly less happy. While we're here, let's not ignore or overlook that there's a huge increase in the number of children diagnosed with attention deficient disorders in this country. If we were to be completely honest with ourselves, this nation of ours is suffering not only from a financial deficit but an attention deficit as well.

We also are suffering from loneliness. Despite the fact that we are all interconnected, 76% of middle-aged Americans report that they have moderate to high levels of loneliness. This loneliness is not a brief subjective state, it also impacts our bodies—our physical and mental health. Recent research shows that loneliness is actually a more significant predictor by more than double the magnitude of early deaths compared to obesity. So this imposes a great toll on your brain as well as your body.

Now let's address negative self-talk and depression, shall we? We all have a narrative in our mind that we carry around about who we are, and sometimes you can have negative beliefs about yourself which can peak depression. This turns out to be a very serious problem, because depression is on the rise. If you look at the shift over the past few years you'll notice a very large increase in depression, especially in women. Over the last three years alone there has been a 33% increase in diagnoses of major depression in women. This shift is accruing in teens as well. But research shows that you can actually train your mind and harness the power of becoming more resilient to the negative feelings you tend to think about yourself.

One pillar to a healthy mind is by simply being more connected to your inner self, mind, body, and soul. Connections refer to those qualities that nurture a sweet, pleasant interpersonal relationship. Qualities like appreciation, being kind, being compassionate in regards to others, and having an overall positive outlook toward life in general. It doesn't take much to start activating these inactive qualities which you can develop to become stronger.

Another way to support a healthy state of mind is having insight about the narrative you tend to think about yourself. At the end of the day there are a lot of people who have a very negative narrative. They have negative self-beliefs, and they hold those beliefs to be a true description of who they are. That, in itself is a true prescription for self-depression. A healthy mind requires changing our relationship to this narrative. Not so much as changing the narrative itself but changing our relationship to it, so that we can look at the narrative and see it for what it truly is. This narrative that I speak of is just a gathering of thoughts. When you can see it as just that, you can promote more breathing room within your mentality which then leads to a healthier well-being.

These next two supports for a healthier mind I purposely saved because I spoke about them in previous chapters. The first is awareness, and this includes the capacity to focus our attention to resist distraction. It also includes a quality of knowing what your mind is doing. For instance, have you ever had the experience while reading a book of reading each word on a page, then you may read every word on the next page, but after a few minutes you have absolutely no idea what you've just read? Don't be alarmed because I, too, have done this plenty of times but that's an example of a lapse of awareness. Now the moment you recognize that you were lost and come back that is the moment of awareness. Awareness is crucial, and actually it's necessary for real transformation to occur.

The next support is finding or having a purpose. Here I'm talking about having a sense that your life is headed in a particular direction. Most importantly, it's about taking more of the activities in your life as belonging to a sense of purpose. Can you envision living your life where simple things, such as taking out the garbage and doing the laundry is still related to your sense of purpose? Being able to broaden it this way is a very crucial ingredient in the recipe for a healthy mind. Have you ever tried training your mind? I've come to learn that there are two different foundational ways of learning. One form of learning is expressed as "declarative learning," which is learning about things. You can learn the value of kindness by reading a book about kindness, but this wouldn't necessarily lead you to become kinder. You can be taught the value of honesty, but this would not necessarily make you an honest person. In order to grow these qualities you need a second form of learning, and that is called "procedural learning." These types of learning operate through different brain circuits, and you need both to produce a real transformation. You see, the wiring in your brain is not fixed its adaptable and you can grasp the power to change your brain. Our brains can change in a remarkably fast period of time. Now, it doesn't mean that these changes will last, but it means that they can occur, that they can begin and with a systematic practice they will endure.

So if you had to start somewhere I highly recommend that you start with just a few minutes a day. It can be while you're commuting to or from work, while brushing your teeth in mornings, during your first cup of coffee or tea, or even as you're walking. This can be incorporated in the day-to-day routines of your life. But through the suggestions I expressed earlier, you can cultivate a strong sense of purpose, you can reduce distraction, and you can increase productivity and focus.

Now believe it or not, your nutrition and what you consume plays a role in your mental stability (hence, you are what you eat), as well as your surroundings. Your physical and psychological health can very well be easily managed if you are in touch with nature, water, soil, light, and things like that. The more exposed you are to healthy behaviors, the more balanced you become both physically and psychologically. There are only four things with you right now that you need to make use of: your body, your mind, your emotions, and your energy. If you manage these four things, they will produce a leveled mental state of mind. Inner energy caters to bringing in great shape to your physical stability, emotional stability and, overall, your mental peace and joy.

CHAPTER 7

Knowledge of Being Yourself

"Are you living or just existing?"
—Tyler Perry

If you sat back and asked yourself "who am I?" what would that answer sound like? If I were to ask, "Who are you?" what would your answer be? I wanted to start this chapter with these specific questions because many of us fail to realize who we are. A large percentage of today's population is living beneath their means and they don't realize it. We fail to realize our worth, our value, who we are, and what physical or mental talent we possess to contribute as our purpose in existing.

Chances are you've looked in at least one mirror today. You've had to shave, or comb your hair, or maybe you had to check your teeth for lettuce after lunch, but what you aren't realizing is that the face looking back at you isn't the face that everyone else sees. The difference is, when you're looking into a mirror you're usually looking for reassurance. You're looking for reassurance that you are beautiful, you're looking for signs of aging, looking to see if you're clean and tidy, or checking your figure or the way you look in a particular outfit. What if you change the focus from looking at yourself to looking for yourself? You would then look for revelation versus reassurance.

When you look at impressive individuals and when I say impressive or successful individuals, I don't mean financially successful, I mean people who have been successful at achieving whatever it is they set out to do. You'll find that the thing they all have in common is that they have nothing in common. These are people who work in many of the fields you work in. They work in corporations, they're heads of various industries, selected politicians, labors to skilled tradesmen, dancers, and even pop stars. These are the ones that are linked by the same thread. These are individuals who've managed to figure out the unique gift that the universe gave them when they personified and then instilled that in the service of their goals. I think that we were all born complete. We come complete with one true note we were destined to sing, and these are people who have managed to figure that out. It doesn't dictate your choice of job, it dictates how you do it. When we see these people, we always call or look at them as larger than life. Then I think how can one be larger than life when life is so large? It's that the majority doesn't take up the space the universe intended for us. This is why when you see someone in the full flow of their humanity, it's remarkable. They appear bigger in every direction than normal human beings and they shine, they glisten, they glow. Throughout my life all of the experiences I've endured have led me to believe that individuality is really all that it's cracked up to be. In fact people who are frightened to be themselves will work for those who aren't afraid. Now your job is not to be anything like any of the people that you may idolize or admire, in fact your job is to be as unlike them as you can possibly be. Your only job while you're here on this planet is to be as good at being you as they are at being them. That's the key.

So let me start here by asking you an incredibly personal question. As a matter of fact this is a question that's been looking for you your whole life. Who do you think you are? It's probably the most simple, yet complicated question you'll ever ask. Yet how many times in your life has somebody offered you that well-meaning piece of advice that you should just be yourself? How many times have you said that to somebody else? One of your

75

kids may come to you, a co-worker, or someone on your team and they tell you they're nervous or scared. They have to go and do something and then their confidence goes away and you say, "Just be yourself and give it all you've got, because when you're yourself, you're incredible, you got this!" It always resonates because that's all we want to do. If you tell Mark to be himself, he doesn't know how to be Paul, Kevin, or Susan, he's quite happy just being himself. But it's the use of the word "just" that's very interesting here for two reasons: (1) it implies that being yourself is an easy thing to do, and (2) it acts as an original word of advice, since Mark had never thought about being himself.

When it comes to being yourself and being in the world the minute you came into your human form, you were given a life sentence. Now you don't know how long you have. Maybe Mark has 65 years, Paul has 73 years, Kevin gets 55 years, and Susan receives 38 years. The point is we have no idea how long we have. Although where you're born, when you're born, and to whom you're born—all of these things have certain influence or impact on how you become who you become. Consequently, if you were born in or to a higher class society of this world, you have a lot more time to figure this out. However, if you were born in or to a lower class of society, you would have significantly less time of a life (no kidding around).

What I want you to think about is not what your life expectancy is but, rather, what do you expect from life? What does life expect from you? Those are more interesting questions. One of the times in your life when you are awesome at being yourself is childhood. When you are a kid you're fantastic at being yourself, because you don't yet know how to disguise your differentness. That's why you can see kids running around the beach naked until suddenly they reach an age where they want a bathing suit or a bikini. Imagine if you walk into a classroom full of four-year-old children. Let's say it's a classroom full of little boys, and you ask, "Who's the strongest boy in the class?" What's going to happen? Every single hand in the class will go up. They'll be competitively strong. If you go into the same classroom that's now full of eight-year-old boys and ask the same question, they'll point and say "him," because they know by that age he's the strongest, he's the fastest runner, he's the funny guy, and he's the bully.

Society's developing of us usually starts about the ages between five and eight years old. That's why the saying goes, "Give me a boy until the age of seven, and I'll show you the man," because that's the birth of consciousness, and from then on you become more self-conscious and, by default, less good at being yourself. The other place you're fantastic at being yourself is when you're old and wrinkled, simply because you get to that stage in your life when you realize there are more summers behind you than in front of you, and everything intensifies. You become more frank, more brutally honest, you become less compromising. So you're going to tell people what you don't want, what you're not going to eat or do, who and what you don't like. Things like, "I don't like that type of music, shut that noise off and, while I'm at it, I don't much like you either." We would in turn call these people abnormal, or irregular when in fact what they're doing is being authentic. It's kind of like an hour glass effect. When you're young, you're great at being yourself, and when you're old, you're great at being yourself, but it's the bit that's in the middle that's the most problematic part. That's the bit where you have to socialize, you have to accommodate, you have to adapt.

Now, you'll see that there are the different complexes that instigate the making of who you are. You're very familiar with the superiority complex. If you have a superiority complex, you pretty much think you're the most important person in building. If you've got an inferiority complex, you may suffer from an overly modest self- importance. These are both signs of a fragile ego. One of them is about a delusion of magnificence, and the other is about delusions of insignificance. However, there's a third way about being in the world, and it's called interiority. The word interiority describes a particular character, and in two reasons it may be useful to you. Number one it's your inner character. If you have a superiority complex or an inferiority complex, you need other people around. For a superiority complex, you need people to be smaller. For an inferiority complex, you need to suffer from the, I'm bound to be exposed syndrome by others that need to find you out or expose you. An interiority complex is something none-relative, so to operate from this position of interiority, it's like an insight point of view. It's a sensibility. It's an alignment, and it'll be the only place in your life that you have no competition. Try and find a comparison to yourself, and I bet you draw a blank.

The famous platinum selling, Grammy award-winning R&B singer, song writer, model, poet, and actress Jill Scott once had to take the stage after the famous songwriter, record producer, actress and four-time Grammy award-winning Erykah Badu. As she was taking the stage, a French filmmaker who was filming her at the time had a question, and so he asked her, "Are you nervous, you know, going on after Erykah?" Jill Scott responded after a soft chuckle by saying, "Have you ever seen me perform?" We all have our own thing, that's the magic, and everyone comes with their own sense of strength, and their own queendom. Mine could never compare to hers, and hers could never compare to mine."

When I speak of interiority, that's what it looks and sounds like. When you figure out how to be yourself, it's an incredibly liberating untragic way to go through life. You don't develop an identity that's based on an out-of-place personality. You're not a blend or a combination of all your experiences and influences. You're not just somebody's boss, or somebody's parent, or anybody's anything. You're yourself. However, chances are there are at least four of you out there in this world, so allow me to introduce yourselves.

The most visible "you" that you represent to the outside world is perception, what everybody else thinks of you, and there are as many opinions of you as there are people. I want you to imagine you're like a big USB stick that you plug in, and you show up on the desktop of the world. That's the power of context. If you don't understand that bit, then being yourself can be an ill-advised strategy. So, of course, it's important that you understand perception, but one of the things I've noticed in terms of gender is there are very few things that I think are gender-specific, but one of them is something called approval addiction. The need to be liked, the need for approval, or acceptance, or recognition, or for someone to tell you it's okay. It may seem that more women suffer from that disorder than men, and I think it's one of the most draining aspects of self-esteem. When it comes to being yourself, needing other people's approval, loving somebody else's opinion and mistaking it for your own is one of the most weakening things you'll do on the road to being yourself. You will never ever be perception-less, but it's important to be perception-free. One of things that's going to help you be perception-free is persona.

This is your wish image. This is what you would like everyone else to think of you, and it's not about being fake, or a fad, or pretending. It's about moving, it's about possibility, it's about potential, it's about belief in yourself. So while there's a part of you that's like your backbone, this part of you would be more like your wish bone. This one is your adaptive personality, your constructive self and even that's unique, because nobody in the world has had the same experiences or influences that you have. But this is the you that keeps moving, that keeps changing all the time. It helps you avoid being one of those people, the people who say to you, "I have 15 years of experience" when in fact they really mean one year, 15 times. They literally repeat themselves year, after year, after year. What I want you to think about with every passing year is your job is to be better, and better at being who you already are. This is not a beautifying exercise, you're already different. Your job is to figure out how, and then to be more of that. Now there are certain times in your life that will lend itself to change, which makes this change quicker and deeper. It's called intervals of possibility. There's not always a sign posted, but there are times in your life when you come to a split in your path, and you sense the potential for change is increased. You meet a stranger in the bar, or at the club, and you have to decide what you're going to do. Your boss comes to you and offers you a new job. What do you want to do? Do you want to keep doing the same thing, or do you want this job? But you know that if you make that change the speed of your life will change. Unfortunately some of these interventions, some of these intervals of possibilities are disastrous, in fact, most of them are tragic because most of us would rather continue sleepwalking until something happens to wake us up. What will happen is the health of someone you love will start to deteriorate, or maybe you'll get sick, or you'll get fired. Maybe it'll take something more impersonal to happen like 9/11, or hurricane

Katrina, or the 1989 earthquake. But something will happen that will rock you back into that inner self and make you ask yourself the question I asked you in the beginning of this chapter. The problem is when it happens catastrophically, you're vulnerable, you're weak. Then it becomes a case of why wouldn't you ask yourself those questions when you're strong? While you have a job, when you're loved. That's when the questions become most useful. So the question on this one is, "If you could be the person of your dreams, who would you be?" The thing that may stop you from being the person of your dreams is what you think of you, your ego.

So now you've got what others think of you, what you would like others to think of you, and what you think of you. But you have good days and bad day's, right? There are days when you wake up and you feel capital, then there are days when you can't even look in the mirror and all you want to do is stay in bed, and even your cell phone becomes a burden. So on the days when you wake up feeling so energized and capital, it's like you've got a reason. It's like free floating joy all throughout your body, and you know how it feels on those days because, you think, "Somebody just give me an audience. I'm on fire. Quick, point me somewhere and tell me when to go—it's show time." You're looking and feeling good, and everything just works on those days. But on the other days nothing seems to work. Your legs don't work, your mouth doesn't work, and you're at a loss of words. It's like your vocabulary has been stolen away from you. Those are two extremes of your ego, and one of them is about self-congratulations, and the other is about self-discipline. Now, I don't care who you are, and I don't care how old you are, your entire life from birth up until now has been about building a stable relationship with your ego. You need an ego to live in

81

a capitalist world. If you didn't have an ego, you'd get cooked. But your challenge is to take the ego from its dominant position and pull it back so that it's in service of yourself. That's when it becomes useful. In order to do that, you've got to find the still point right in the middle of these two extremes, and that is what I would call self-composure or self-balance. It's the kind of state of mind that cannot be affected in any way by anything that happens outside of you. This kind of confidence that comes from there is like the confidence of the sky. Right now it's dark outside but you know that if you went up in an airplane even on the stormiest days, the sky is blazing blue underneath. So when you look at this sky and it has made a rainbow and it's gorgeous in its own right, there's no question that the sky's up there going, "Yeah, you see my rainbow?" Now when it's a terrible, gray, and gloomy type of day, the sky's not going to apologize. No, the sky just is, because the sky sees the importance of clouds. The sky sees the uncertainty of the clouds and the uncertainty of the rainbows, and you have to develop an inner state of mind that is as fluctuating as all the good and bad that happens to you—just as the sky is to the weather. Now this feeling would also be called a feeling of humility. Humility is not thinking less of yourself, humility is thinking about yourself less.

The last you, is the ever present unchanging you. This is the you, that you have been since you were around seven years old, and the you that you would be when you reach 97 or older (God willing). Your life is your message. You must make your life your message. Otherwise, why are you here? It's not like you have a spare and in comparison to the video games I used to play, it's not like you can just click the restart button and try again. So when you think about your identity, when you think about what it means to be alive, when you think about why you deserve to exist, you're not your thoughts, because you think them. You can't be your feelings, because otherwise who's the you that feels them? You're not what you possess, and you're not what you do, you're not even who you love, or who loves you. There has to be something underneath all that. When you look at people who have managed to transcend all the judgments that we place upon them. Even when you're born without many of the attributes that some of your siblings or peers may have. Even when you're born in a way that may lead you to feel powerless, useless or inadequate. If you can tap in to that inner voice that I've been talking about, you might just end up being at 12 years old, the youngest person ever called to the National World Champion swim, track or basketball team. You might even end up at the age of 13 being the youngest ever Olympian gold medal winner. You might even end up at 14 being the youngest person ever to get a CGM (Congressional Gold Medal). That's what happens when you dial in to your personal direct objective. So if you can do this, not only will the speed of your life get quicker, not only will the substance of your life get richer, but you would never feel unneeded again.

The questions you ask yourself will determine your life. Instead of asking yourself, "What do I need to do to get rich?" ask yourself, "What could I do and love every day, even if I were failing?" Life is too short; this is your one go-round, so what are you going to do? You're going to build a life that's predicated around value. You're going to build a life predicated on passion. This piece of mind comes once you realize that it's not about who you are today, but that it's about whom you want to become and the price you're willing to pay to get there.

What I've learned on this incredible journey of mine are a few undeniable truths about what enables us to succeed. One is that fear exists, and the only thing you can do is face it. If not, it can prevent you from growing, so it's better to embrace it. The second is that self-confidence is huge. It's very important, and you've got to work on it every day of your awakening life. The third is (and I'm glad we discussed it in previous chapters) that you've got to live your life with purpose. If you don't have purpose in your life, you don't have momentum. You don't have anything driving you forward; you don't have anything pulling you out of bed every single day. I promise you the day that you're willing to pay any price to succeed, you'll achieve what you want to achieve. If you truly believe that your potential is limitless, what do you want to become? Then ask yourself what price are you willing to pay to get there?

CHAPTER 8

Knowledge of Being Observant

"The fact is, the public have an insatiable curiosity to know everything, except what is worth knowing."
—Oscar Wilde

Eighty-five percent of communication is nonverbal. Research has shown that back in 1993 students could correctly identify the quality of a teacher they had never seen before by watching just 10 seconds of the class with the sound turned down. Their results matched very closely to the qualities said by those who have been students of these same teachers for a whole year. I have witnessed many times in my life, people allowing opportunities to pass them by through the lack of paying attention. I have seen more times than I can count those who become victims of circumstances due to not being aware, and we've seen on the news, social media even hearsay of the tragic stories that could have, should have, and would have been avoided if that particular person were cautious of their surroundings. In this chapter I'm going to break down the power of being observant—how observation can be an asset to your life versus a liability—and teach you ways to become more observant.

Besides nature in its entirety, humans and human ideology makes the world go around (figuratively speaking). For this reason I feel you can learn from every human being, living or dead, to become successful or unsuccessful. Through thorough observation you can learn either what to do or what not to do. I believe if we make more frequent observations and filter what we are observing appropriately, the world could and would be a place full of more ideas, comfort, and understanding. It happens that we now are living in an age of information. In this informative age we have access to lots and lots of information, but we don't always observe the right things. Observation can be used as a tool to shed light on darkness, to find a problem that you're passionate about, and to see the beauty that will inspire you to take action. It's not always about knowing everything if you want to make a difference in the world, it's about knowing the valuable things and a willingness to live and die for them.

Observation is a whole brain activity. It's about paying attention to detail, focus, analyzing, reasoning, and memory. Some of the benefits you get out of razor-sharp observation skills are that you become more aware, you become smarter, your job performance as well as your relationships improve. It's a highly important skill, but what's even better is it can be sharpened by meditating. When you can maintain a clear mind with no thoughts bothering you, this is the state when you get direct access to heavenly energy. Reaching this state sharpens your attention, gives you better focus, your mental processing becomes faster, and your memory becomes stronger. If meditating isn't one of your strong points, start with something simple. Try to remember the events of the day. In the evening when you make it back home from your day's work and after you have freshened up, relax in a chair, close your eyes, and try to recall the day's events. Visualize all the details as they had happened. Stay with the picture and make them as real as you can. These exercises will make your memory stronger and help you with your observation skills.

Trial and error—anything worth doing is worth doing unsuccessfully. Remember the time when you were trying to learn how to ride a bicycle? Did you ride it down the street the very first time you got on it? I highly doubt it. What most likely happened was you failed. You're taking off and braking was awful, and you probably fell a couple of times. But when you kept working at it, suddenly you got it. You were able to ride, and it became so smooth and effortless. The thrill you got became mind blowing, the feeling was out of this world for your younger self. Now, just like that first lesson on the bicycle, your observation skills may be bad initially, but as you keep working on it you get better and better. Take any skill, for instance, when you first start you are a bit clumsy, awkward, and not sure of yourself. But as you keep at it, eventually you master it.

I'm going to take the time here to express how and the importance of being able to read and observe people. Sometimes we get mixed signals. Maybe our intuition, our perception, or past experiences makes us not the best at reading people. Thankfully all is not lost, and we can get better at reading people, but how and at what expense? I'll start by mentioning something I'm quite sure we all are familiar with or have at least heard once in our lives, and that's listening to your gut. The majority of people don't trust their gut feelings. Have you ever been in a position of having to make a decision and your gut is telling you one thing, your heart is telling you something else, and your mind is telling you something completely different from what your gut and your heart are saying. I've literally been in situations where I had over thought myself into a bad purchase, bad situation, or lengthy sentence when my gut was telling me exactly what to do, but my heart or mind said different. We usually trust our brains and believe what our brain tells us to believe. A study from the University of California shows that people only recognize lies 43% of the time and truths 48% of the time when trusting their brains. When trusting their gut, the accuracy rate is way higher. Trust your gut because your intuitions aren't going to lie, and first impressions are often accurate.

Observe people. Paying attention to others more than you pay attention to yourself is a quick tip to becoming more observant. This is important in observation, because at this stage you are trying to observe the world and not yourself. As a great observer, you have to get great at noticing the world around you, and not the world within you. It may seem difficult and borderline contradicting to the previous chapter, but here is where you separate the difference from the observation of self to observing your surroundings to benefit yourself. Say you wanted to become a dancer, the fastest way to become one is to observe other dancers. The way they move their body, their feet, even their facial expression to their energy. You will always learn how to do something faster by watching other people who are doing it. Once you get it you've got it, then by adding your own twist to it you elevate it. This goes for other things that may appeal to you as well, such as cooking, operating machinery, driving a car, writing code using software, or making a video. Through the observation of people, either living or dead, successful or unsuccessful, you can learn many things like what to and what not to do. You know the old saying, "You can learn a lot from a dummy."

Make it you're business to notice changes. Observe something for a period of time to set a baseline or timeline. You need to find out what is normal in your surroundings so then when things aren't so normal you have something to compare it to, and to reassure you of what had changed from what's usually the same. When you get good at this you'll start to notice when things are out of place, but you should always have a reference point first. Set a baseline for everything and, to make it simple, start with the closest people around you. It can be your family, a co-worker, the mailman, or even the cashier at your local grocery store. The change is what's important. It's not just how someone acts, but how and what makes them change from how they usually act. After you get better by putting in plenty of hours of observing, reading body language becomes second nature, and soon you'll be able to read a whole room. Keeping notice of that person who seems a little tense, agitated, and aggressive may keep you distant from the trouble he's sure to stir up. Noticing those who appear to be a threat and being watchful of their position or location in a room can be the difference between going home or going to the hospital.

Pay attention to people's speech and behavior. The first time you meet some people, they may put up a false persona or try to manipulate your perception of them. This is common when two strangers meet and one is trying to give of the impression of what they feel the other would like or need. Then a little later in the relationship or friendship when the mask has been removed, their false persona has faded away, and the real true person is revealed. It's like you don't even recognize this person you fell in love with, slept next to, and you spent time with. The people who are actually being honest and genuine with you should mimic your words and actions. This shows they're in sync with you and how you're feeling. However, they may also be trying to deceive and mentally penetrate the guards you have put up to protect yourself. In this case pay extra attention to their facial structure. Hold that handshake a little longer while you stare into their eyes and see if they can maintain that eye contact, or if you notice an uncomfortable shift in their demeanor from their first approach. Then you'll be able to determine whether it's genuine sincerity or not.

Body language is a major giveaway to someone's true emotion. If someone's sad, they might suddenly have their head down with a slouch in their shoulders. Are they anxious, sweating or pacing? Are they checking their phone? Maybe they're not into the conversation. Are their smiles just small grins? Pay attention, look deep into a person's eyes. I can't state enough how important it is to pay attention to someone's facial expression. This aspect of a person's body language can be hard for a person to interpret. Sometime each side of the face can give off two different emotions. Some are obvious. An upturned mouth with crow's feet at the eyes usually means its sincere happiness behind that smile. Some emotions are a combination of different signs like embarrassment. When some people are embarrassed they might smile. However the lips are tighter than a happy smile. Lips might also be pulled tight when compassion is felt as opposed to sadness, when the lips are pulled down. While it's confusing, it's important to learn these few signs for a significant advantage for reading people.

Being or showing empathy to those around you may seem obsolete; however, it's very important. Some people have a natural talent for empathizing with others, while others don't. To be able to increase your empathy you need good people-reading and understanding skills. Empathy would help you see things from someone else's perspective and, as a consequence, will allow you to read their emotions and intentions much better.

Pay attention to one's appearance. Making judgments on someone's appearance might feel shallow, but it can say a few things. Take a Sherlock Holmes approach on this matter, notice how that person may be wearing Jordan Prime sneakers, maybe he likes basketball, sports in general, or may be highly involved in the sneaker culture. People's appearance can give you precise hints into their character. Do they wear lots of colors? Are they well-dressed, or very sloppy? These behaviors can give clues about them, such as if they're organized and diligent, or lazy and a slob. If a person hardly cares about themselves you can't expect them to care much about you.

Be open to the objective perspective approach, because all of these tips may lead to some bias. To successfully read someone, enter the situation objectively. Leave your past feelings about that person behind. Focus on what they're saying and how they're behaving in that moment. Your feelings can create a false impression on what they're conveying, especially negative feelings. I have studied this approach so much I'm at the point now where I not only listen to what people say to me, I listen to what they're not saying. You'd be amazed at what you can extract from people by asking them questions against what they say versus what they're not saying.

When observing others, it's in your best interest to have patience. In order to read someone accurately, it takes practice. People are complex. If you're in a conversation with them, they're likely also to pick up on your signs as well. You can't be an instant expert on someone or automatically assume everything about a person. If the communication continues they will open up at their own pace, and that's when you can figure out if you read them correctly or not.

To become a better observer you must separate or put away distractions. How could you notice sudden changes in body language or the size of someone's pupils if your phone has all of your attention? There are all kinds of distractions in this busy world, but if you can laser focus on something you're observing, you'll increase your chances of understanding situations better. You must be careful about where your attention is going. As an observer, it's your duty to make sure that you're investing your attention wisely. Laser focused computed thinking requires dedication to the subject. You'll find it nearly impossible to focus on two subjects and give 100% attention to both. Also putting away distractions gives you an empty mentality. What I mean by this is that your mind will be looking for things to do. It will eventually get bored, the brain's natural state is to wonder, and you would give it a purpose by starting to look for changes or things out of the ordinary in your current or previous surroundings.

Once you are able to make observations with little effort, you can go one step further and learn how to link these observations together to form a bigger picture. You can do this by reasoning backwards. Try to find a conclusion and then think of what you can observe to confirm it. For example if you see someone with a stain on their shirt that looks or resembles marinara sauce, and you notice it's around 1:00 p.m. right after lunch, you can come to the conclusion that maybe they had pizza or spaghetti for lunch. Once you learn to think in this mindset you can observe without the knowledge of conclusion. Test your observation skills. Walk into a room and observe everything, and then walk out of that room and take a pen/pencil and paper and take notes on people's faces, clothes, and objects. The more things you are able to remember means the better your attention, the more you're focused, your mental processing is faster, and your memory muscle is stronger.

What I've come to learn over the years of my life and participation in my extra curricular activities is that you gain a tremendous power by simply observing the world around you. So here and now I want to get through to you that your intellect has nothing to do with your ability to make the world better, or yourself for that matter. It has everything to do with your skills of observation. Because when we can really see the world

92

around us, we can come up with new ideas, ask questions, and be curious. But the magic is in the questions that those questions bring. That's when you get the game-changing ideas, and those ideas will go on to eventually make the world a better place and make yourself a better person. You will be more in demand if your observation skills are sharper. So use your skills to observe people, customers, situations, problems, products, pitfalls, services, team members, and development in technology as well as strategy.

Arguably, to observe is the most important thing in our lives. To acquire knowledge you must study, but to acquire wisdom you must observe. Now where I want to take you may contradict my earlier statements just a little; however, as we all as individuals don't think the same. We all observe in very different ways, and I aim to touch as many mentalities as applicable. So with that being said, let's look at observing without any distortion.

I want you too learn the art of observing without any distortion, without any motive, without any purpose—just to observe. In observing there is immense beauty because there is no misrepresentation, no twisting up the facts. You see things clearly as they are. It's when you make a distraction of your observation into an idea and then through that it becomes a distortion. So you are purely, freely without any distorted factors entering your observation by simply observing consciousness. Consciousness then begins to reveal itself in its own totality. There's nothing hidden. It is what some would call content, which is our hurt, our greed, our envy, our beliefs, our happiness, our ideologies. All that makes up consciousness—the past, the present scientific or factual traditions, and so on. To observe it without any judgment or movement of thoughts, because when you're thoughts occur it says to you "This is right, this is wrong, this should be and that shouldn't." You're still within the field of consciousness and you're not going beyond it. So you would have to understand very clearly, the place of your thoughts. Thoughts have their own place, and that's in the field of knowledge, technology and all of that.

When you step out of the place of observing consciousness and into the field of observation through thoughts, that's when things become confusing or even contradicting. So then the question becomes, "Can you observe without any movement of thought interfering with your observation?" It is only possible when the observer realizes that what you are observing is you as the observer, and you are also being observed. Anger becomes you when you are angry; you are jealousy when you become jealous, so there's no division between the observer and the observed. That is the basic reality you must capture. You must understand that the reality of thoughts are not truth, they're simply thoughts.

We all need to observe more rather than go with our personal reactions. The more you observe, the less you entertain or enter into foolishness. We are so much in our actions, interactions, and reactions and less into observing. It's almost as if observing is given very little to no importance. Many great discoveries have come through being silent, observing, and not allowing your attention to get carried away. The simple act of observing allows you to be grounded, relying on your natural trust, your confidence, openness, and so on. Being observant can help you stay ahead of the curve or, even better, helps you create the curve.

CHAPTER 9

Knowledge of Adaptability & How to Adapt

"Change is the only constant in life.
One's ability to adapt to those changes
will determine your success in life."
—Benjamin Franklin

"I cannot control the direction of the wind, but I can
adjust my sails to always reach my destination."
—Jimmy Dean

One of many quotes I like says, "Adaptability is about the powerful difference between adapting to cope and adapting to win," by Max McKeown. Since I spoke on the knowledge and the power of observation in the previous chapter, I'll follow up with the knowledge, power, and importance of adapting to those changes you observe, as well as the importance of how and why they play a key part in becoming the greatest you. Have you ever found yourself in a situation in which it seems like you've finally got everything squared away and you've figured everything out, but all of a sudden your situation changes? Well don't be alarmed or become overwhelmed, it's just nature's way of telling you it's time to reevaluate, readjust, and encouraging you to grow. In this chapter we are going to explore adaptability and how to adapt not only to survive but to conquer.

We are all introduced to change the day we are born. We make space, we change relationships, and we change lives as we make room for ourselves thorough our exposure to change. We build our mental system to what has changed over a period of time. There are people out there that have a great mental system, and they adapt to change without a problem. There are also people who adapt to change over a period of time through experiences and age, and there are people who are totally scared of the word change based on how powerful change is and can be.

Our world is constantly changing and evolving, and if you're not able to change with it then you'll be ultimately left behind. Adaptability is being able to rapidly learn new skills and behaviors in response to a changing of environment and circumstances. This is true in every aspect of our lives, whether it be our physical conditions, family, friendships, or our professional life. Our economy is changing all the time, and businesses need to respond and adapt to the change to be able to stay in the game. Trends come and go, and people constantly change their personal preferences. You just have to possess the ability to be ready when or how change happens. Adaptability is equally important from one aspect of your life to the other. When utilized accordingly, it can give you the advantage over co-workers, competitors, and the oppositions. People generally don't like change because it requires more effort than doing things the same old way they've been doing things for years. For this reason people try to resist change whenever possible, but doing things in the same way comes with the same results but, more importantly, at the cost of growth and new opportunities. Every time you avoid trying a new strategy or approach, you are missing out on better ways of doing things or bettering yourself. So you have to start embracing change in your life and, as you do, you'll be surprised to see what progress you're making.

Think of a moment in your life when something so impactful has shaped your journey to where you are today or contributed to it in some form. Change, when it happens is what you were thinking in that moment, and chances are you remember when it happened, exactly what you were doing when it happened, and how it impacted you once it happened. That is the point of the origin of change and why being able to adapt to it is so powerful. Change comes in two forms, it can be planned or it can be unplanned. Planned change is simple. It's the feeling of a need or want, and the desire to change something in your life. You actually initiate the change and bring it into action; however, the results can be totally unexpected. When it comes to unplanned change—that's a little more difficult. It usually comes in stages of denial, then acceptance, to managing your life according to what has changed and, finally, growth from that occurrence of change. For example, any dis-attachment from a loss of time spent in a broken relationship can be easily repaired, and that valuable experience you have while you're repairing it becomes priceless. Do not let it go to waste, because you don't know who's watching you, and you don't know who's going to cross your path in life and actually learn from you. But, more importantly, the point at which you have that valuable experience prepares you for the next unexpected change that life is sure to throw at you.

I've gone through so much change in my life, and at this stage in my life I find it to be fascinating. From the spontaneous outbursts of violence in the households I grew up in, to my mom moving me from East Palo Alto, CA, where all of my friends and family lived, to the city of Hayward, CA, where I found myself labeled as an outsider. I was incarcerated in various institutions, from juvenile detention to the state penitentiary. I told myself I'll never work for anybody, to me rather working for somebody than to risk going back to prison. I became a father balancing parenthood, as well as becoming an entrepreneur entertaining numerous entities and business ventures. Trust me, I've had my fair share of adapting and readjusting. I will admit that adapting wasn't easy, but it was definitely doable, always necessary, and undoubtedly in my best interest. Overall it was worth it.

When it comes to adapting, why do we as individuals do it differently? Some people easily adapt while others clearly struggle. If we look at the reality of our global economy, then we could agree that the pace of change isn't slowing down. It's estimated that 80% of the jobs that will exist in 2030 aren't the same jobs that exist today. The average number of jobs people have in their lifetime is now 12, and in 12 different companies. That's a lot of change, and given that one-third of America's workforce is at this moment dealing with a case of anxiety or mental health issues only confirms that we are not coping very well with what's going on. We are losing the ability to react productively and, based on this, I believe we have to do better with change. We're not allowing the time and attention it takes to prepare and develop ourselves. The world around us is constantly jumping from change to change, and we're acting on impulse verses through strategy. The purpose of this chapter is to help you respond to change the way you want to, and to be the person you want to become through change.

Have you ever found yourself asking if you would be able to adapt to a new circumstance, or have you experienced a difficult situation that life has thrown at you and found it hard to cope? In this world of ours, we must be able to blend in at will like a chameleon, or change with the circumstances like an Arctic fox, which can be white in the winter yet brown in the summer. The ability to do this is very important due to the fact that the world we live in continuously goes through changes. As I have grown up pay phones have been replaced by cellular phones, and road maps have been replaced by Google Maps or MapQuest. Taxi cab services have been replaced by Uber or Lyft, and consumer shopping has become convenient through the use of Amazon. Just compare life in the 1960s to life in the 1980s to life in the 2000s, and imagine what's to come. We are all living through and experiencing a conversion of forces happening now, which is unparalleled in the history of the world we were used to. Whether it's through artificial intelligence (AI), virtual reality (VR), robotics, or industrialized sourcing, things are changing and at a rapid pace. Because of this alone my assertion is that the world is looking for people who can adapt, and those who can't or won't will be left behind.

It's not always easy to respond to change the way you want to. Through comfort, predictability, and practicality adaptability may become to some people a burden. We all struggle to adapt sometimes, and quite often the coping mechanisms that we had in the past don't necessarily work in the future. As we progress into leaders, parents, and mature human beings, we need to be even more aware of how we adapt to change. We've been conditioned to live our lives in the midst of so much change and urgency and, consequently, we respond and we react instinctively. We react to what's in front of us because we have to, but we don't take the time to prepare ourselves in advance of a change.

You can have an high IQ (intelligence quotient), which is a measure of a person's reasoning ability, or a high EQ (emotional quotient), which is the ability to understand, use, and manage your own emotions in positive ways to relieve stress, communicate effectively, empathize with others, overcome challenges, and defuse situations. But you would still need to be equipped with the ability to be adaptable. Adapting is your ability to adjust and how well you react to the inevitability of change. I subscribe to the belief that adaptability itself is a form of intelligence and your

AQ (adaptability quotient), which is something that can be tested and improved upon. Your AQ is increasingly important because the world is speeding up. We know that the rate of technological change is accelerating and is forcing our brains to react to it, whether you're navigating changing job conditions brought on by AI, shifty politics for a more globalized world, or personal relationships. All of us as individuals, groups, corporations, or even governments are being forced to tussle with more change than ever before in human history.

So how do you assess your adaptability? For starters you can ask yourself "what if" questions to hypothetically prepare yourself if such a situation should arrive. These "what if" questions should sound something like, "What if my house caught on fire, what would be the exit plan for my family and me?" "What if a natural disaster occurs, such as an earthquake, tornado, or hurricane and knocked out the power or destroys our property, how would we fend for ourselves?" "What if I were to get fired, what would my next step be?" "What if our country suffered an unexpected pandemic (or plandemic) and everyday items at the store are no longer available, how would I care, provide, and supply for my family or myself?" Asking yourself the "what ifs" forces the brain to simulate; it forces the brain to picture multiple possible versions of the future. The strength of that vision, as well as how many distinct scenarios you can come up with, helps you navigate through life.

Practicing simulations is a safe testing ground for improving adaptability. It can mentally prepare you for a worst-case scenario because, as you know like I know, life happens. Instead of testing how you take in and retain information (like an IQ test might), it assesses how you manipulate information given a restriction in order to achieve a certain goal.

I'm going to share a story as an example about someone who programmed his bicycle to turn left when he steered right, and vice versa. He called it his backward brain bike, and it took him nearly eight months to learn how to ride it sort of normally. The fact that he was able to unlearn how to ride his regular bike, in favor of a newly remodeled one, exposes something that's fascinating about our adaptability—that it's not so fixed. Instead, you have the capacity to improve it through dedication and hard work.

There's a sort of natural tension between exploitation and exploration and collectively we all tend to over value exploitation. Here's an example. In the year 2000 a man finessed his way into a meeting with John Antioco, the former CEO of Blockbuster Video, and proposed a partnership to manage Blockbuster's nested online business. The Blockbuster CEO laughed the man out of the room saying, "I have millions of existing customers and thousands of successful stores, and I really need to focus on the money." The other man in the meeting, however, turned out to be Reed Hastings, the co-founder and executive chairman of Netflix. In 2018 Netflix brought in 15.8 billion dollars. Blockbuster filed for bankruptcy in 2010, exactly 10 years after that meeting. The former Blockbuster CEO was too focused on exploiting his already successful business model, so much so that he couldn't see around the next corner. In that way his previous success became the enemy of his potential to adapt. Never fall to far in love with your wins, but rather continue to proactively seek out what might be the next successful opportunity.

When I first started exploring adaptability, the thing I found interesting is that you can improve it. You have the capacity to become more adaptable. But think of it like a muscle, because it has to be exercised. Don't get discouraged if it takes awhile. Over time using the strategies that I explained earlier, asking yourself "what if" questions, actively unlearning to re-learn, and prioritizing exploration over exploitation can put you in the driver's seat so that next time something big changes you're already prepared. We're entering a future in which IQ and EQ both matter way less than how fast you're able to adapt. So I hope that what I've explained helps you to raise your own AQ.

You can't always control the change that happens to you, but you can manage your response to it. I've found that people who are able to be adaptable, who can respond to change how they want to, have this certain adaptability, this certain characteristic about them in common. For those who struggle to adapt, those same characteristics were minimal or just plain missing. To give it an identity I'm going to call it the adaptability recipe. This recipe consists of purpose, habitual curiosity, resilience, and threat. Developing your capabilities in this area can help you become more adaptable.

Let's look at the first ingredient, which is purpose. A wise man once said you'll never reach your destination if you stop and throw stones at every dog that barks. Those with a strong purpose know that it's actually their purpose that will help them weather the storm without getting distracted or demotivated. It helps them to be more adaptable, because it's their purpose that guides them to make the right decisions and choices in the face of change. Let's look at founder and CEO of Tesla Motors, Elon Musk. People credit him for the design of electric vehicles, but his purpose is to rid the world of carbon admissions. Today he chooses electric cars, tomorrow it's solar power or the Hyperloop. His power of purpose is so strong that Tesla is worth more than Ford, Toyota, or GMC motor companies even though it never made a profit until the year 2020. I have described the importance of purpose, and I pray that you have discovered yours, but did you know everyday habits and choices will take you to it, or it can push it further away?

Habitual curiosity is that inner child that asks a million and one questions a day. It requires space and a certain mindset to constantly learn and grow. This characteristic is people's constant ability to scan their environment looking for the need to adapt in the future. This makes them more adaptable, because all the powerful thinking and insight that's happened before the change hits them before they decide to make the change. Think about it—the more questions you ask the more you learn, and the more you learn the more questions you think of to ask. It's a reinforcing cycle. So think about a problem in a different way, try a new solution, and ask stupid questions. When you find yourself facing a new situation, first understand and know that you're not the only one who has encountered some form of this situation, and you most certainly won't be the last. Take the time out to ask yourself, "What questions can I ask that will give me the knowledge and understanding to help me better deal with and adapt to this situation. Nobody wants to feel left alone or that they're without any hope. It wouldn't hurt to find someone who has similarly experienced it, done it and overcame it.

I discovered there's this characteristic of overcoming setbacks and reducing stress, both for individuals and those around them, and this I call resilience. It's been proven that the formation of a habit is not affected by falling off the wagon every now and then. So that cake you ate while being on a diet, and that day or two you missed going to the gym, or that outburst you had while attempting to work on your self-control are normal and they're expected. It's actually overcoming these setbacks and learning from them that will help you become more adaptable. So be honest with yourself. Have the setbacks and changes you've experienced made you settle for being off course? Or are you still on track to being who you want to be? You need not worry about your future. Fully focus on your todays, because the decisions you make in the present determines your future. When understanding change, it's usually really in three areas , which are things within you, things within your extended environment, and things within your friends or family. So to understand resilience, you need to realize that it's the capacity to withstand or to recover quickly from difficulties or the ability to spring back into shape.

Now these first three characteristics have a positive correlation with adaptability, so developing high capabilities in these areas will help you to become more adaptable. But now were going to speak about a characteristic that has a negative correlation with adaptability. A high level of threat will actually hurt your adaptability overall, and our aim here is to reduce it. We all have a threat response when faced with a real, perceived, or potential danger. This can be due to aggressive body language, a different point of view, or a fear of looking stupid. The effect it has on the brain is the same as being followed down a dark alley. To be highly adaptable you need to have a strong awareness of your threat response—what it looks like, and what it feels like, what triggers it, and how best to manage it.

Historically it was thought that the brain is a physiological static organ, and that it's developed in early childhood and you're just stuck with what you got. While it's true that the brain is much more plastic in the early years, plasticity happens throughout life. We may just need a little bit more focus and persistence as we get older. We are meant to adapt, but the brain is highly efficient and this means it will look for patterns to avoid having to consciously think about the same thing over and over again.

So just like a river flowing down the bank, the brain naturally looks for the easy route, encouraging us into thinking the same way and reacting the same way, creating thinking habits and blind spots. It's much easier for us to continue doing something we have always done than it is to stop. Unless you know this and make a consistent commitment to change, you have the capacity to learn, therefore you have the capability to adapt, you just have to start. Remember, change comes with growth and growth comes with change. The difference in the outcome is you enabling yourself to adapt accordingly. Every single person has experienced a braking in some form.

So the equation would look something like this. Purpose, plus habitual curiousness, plus resilience, divided by threat, equals adaptability. To be highly adaptable and to be able to respond to change, you want to develop the ingredients with the reduction of threat in the adaptability recipe. What's interesting about these characteristics is that they are non-fixed, meaning they're adjustable, they're not genetic so they can be learned over the course of time. I found this interesting because throughout the course of my life, and being incarcerated and exposed to different individuals I had the privilege to encounter, I found that they had not just been adaptable, they had learned to adapt. If you happen to wonder how I was able to come to this conclusion, it was through heavy observation and studying every breathing soul in my surroundings, who could possibly be a danger to my life (hence the knowledge of being observant).

105

CHAPTER 10

Shaking the Fakes

"A great deal of intelligence can be invested in ignorance when the need for illusion is deep."
—Saul Bellow

With life, and I'm sure you heard of this, it's this little concept called misdirection. This is similar to a cognitive psychology called selective attention. What that means is that, at any given moment we are surrounded by a number of things that you either see, hear, fear, smell, and physically touch. But there's so much information around us, it would overload your brain to actually try and process every single detail. So instead your brain is constantly trying to filter out the thing that it perceives to be unimportant, so you can focus on the things that matter the most. Unfortunately we sometimes give our attention to what we think is most important, only to discover that our focus was in the wrong place. In fact, we don't just focus on the wrong things, our brain actually creates illusions of what we are experiencing.

When you are unsure about what's happening or what's about to happen, your brain just makes an assumption and inserts what it thinks you're experiencing or going to experience. For example, if you were about to play an instrument, take a test, play a sport, or even give a presentation, you begin to anticipate how you might perform. These assumptions that are often subconscious might give you a feeling of confidence. They may also leave you feeling anxiety and self-doubt. As a matter of fact, it's completely possible that you can possess the knowledge, expertise, and experience you need to succeed but your brain still tells you you're going to fail. These illusions of failure can keep you from trying new things, engaging in an important conversation, and keep you from doing things that may otherwise normally come natural to you. You can learn to stop these basic illusions.

First you have to instill in your head that what your brain is telling you is an illusion of the only forcible outcomes. You can choose to focus on the illusion of everything that may go wrong, or stop focusing on the illusions and instead see all the possibilities of what may potentially go right. Is there an illusion of an assumption that you view of yourself? Is there an assumption that you have made that has kept you from doing something you know you could do? If so, view all the possibilities of an adventure you just haven't discovered yet. Maybe it's that dream that you've always wanted to chase that you can still hear whispering your name, calling you, just waiting for you to bring it into fruition. It may be possible that you are missing out on your calling because you're focused on the illusion of what might go wrong. Stop the illusions and instead see all the good that could come from making a difficult or unusual decision. Don't look back on your life one day and wonder, "Where did the time go?" Instead choose to be intentional about what happens next.

I wanted to address the issue of illusions and how they may affect of your thinking capacity in regard to it being aligned with the conversation of the topic of shaking what's fake. But now, here's where we're going to shift gears a little while I address the fake in people as well as friends, their intentions, how to identify them, and how to shake them. I'm going to discuss behaviors of the sincere, verses the insincere. Those that are in your best interest, verses those that are not and how to spot them before it's too late.

In order to feed your destiny, you have to be careful about whom you spend your time with or you're going to become like the people you hang around with. If you associate with the wrong types of people, they can feed you doubt, feed you negativity, and feed you gossip. If they're negative, critical, compromised, or they don't have integrity, they're bound to feed into you the wrong things that are not in accordance to your appetite. Life's too precious to be devalued by those who don't appreciate your worth and your time. It's too valuable to be wasted by people who aren't going anywhere, and they do not have your best interests in mind. When you do notice this and seek distance, you don't necessarily have to announce it, just find yourself spending less and less time with them. You might think to yourself, "Well, what if I hurt their feelings?" "What if I cause them to become an enemy by making them upset with me?" My answer to that is "What if you miss out on your destiny?" "What if they're preventing you from reaching the next level?" To simply put it, if you don't get rid of the wrong people, you won't meet the right people, or even worse, you could meet an early demise.

As you can probably tell by now, I don't mind using my own experiences to get my point across. So I'm going to briefly share a story with you that simplified my understanding of friend or foe with regard to what happened to a family member of mine. To make it short, he was stabbed in the heart by his, at the time, "best friend." I was between the 3rd and 4th grades when this happened, so trying to wrap my young mind around someone I call family getting killed by his best friend was confusing and hard to understand. Without getting into details, I couldn't figure out how your best friend could kill you. My thoughts went from, "I couldn't kill any of my friends" to, "With friends like that, who needs enemies?" Shortly afterward, I put family over everything and I had no friends. As you can imagine it caused a lot of confusion for me mentally, but I'd like to think that had this person known the extent of betrayal this so-called friend of his would go to, he would have at least created a bit more space and surveyed him a lot more closely. So growing up I never forgot that lesson in friendships and used it to hone in on my interactions with people. So I'm going to go further into the early signs of detected fake characteristics, how to avoid those fake characters, and how to potentially use them in your own best interest. With this in mind I'm going to start with basic and gradually build up to the fake qualities of a person.

For starters, pay close attention to the personal appearance of a person. Do they groom themselves properly or poorly? Do they keep up on their hygiene and appearance? If someone doesn't care about themselves, they may not care much about you, and this can possibly lead to jealousy, which acts against you. Do they gossip or spread rumors? You best believe if they are talking about others to you, they are definitely talking about you to others. Are they the cause of or enjoy being in the midst of a lot of drama? Someone that's drama-oriented will soon be the cause of you finding yourself in dilemmas you never asked for, or will surely stir up some issues between you and others, because this is what they naturally do. Are they always negative toward your goals and aspirations? This too is a jealousy trait. We all don't think the same, and while someone may be beside you as a friend, they may be insecure, self-conscious, or lack confidence or vision. While you're striving to achieve short-term accomplishments for a long-term goal, they secretly see this doable or possible for them and damn sure don't want to see it as a possibility for you. Or maybe they always seem to be in competition with you. It is one thing to be friendly competitive to build each other up, but it's another to always want to outdo or out shine you.

Understand that someone being fake with you won't support your vision or your way of life, putting you down and offering negative feedback toward every idea you may have. They'll say things like "You can't do that!" "That idea sounds impossible." "I don't even see the point, you should try something else." They'll mock your desire to improve your situation. They'll give you a long list of people who failed to do things you're attempting to do, followed by the suggestion that you shouldn't even try, and give you reasons why you should give up. It's the friends who uplift you and want to see you on top that you need to surround yourself with. Somebody being real with you would without the slightest hesitation call you out on your B.S., and support when you're doing something right. If they don't encourage you to pursue your goals and instead insist on putting you down, you've got a fake friend on your hands. This would most likely be the best sign when diagnosing your friend relationship.

Another negative sign is when an acquaintance will put their personal pride over the relationship the two of you may have. They won't step up, apologize or take accountability when they are wrong. Real friends know when they're wrong, and are strong enough to embrace it. They will accept that they made a mistake and apologize for their acts of behavior or comments made. Real friends will discuss the events that led up to the issue and the friendship will come out stronger.

A fake friend will talk about other people behind their backs. I couldn't express this enough. As I stated earlier, it's a fact that if they gossip to you about your other friends when they're not around, they gossip about you to those friends when you're not around. If someone is a real friend, they'll never want to stir up drama among friends for the sake of it, especially in the circle of friends that you care about. Gossip for the sake of drama is a sign of emotional immaturity, and people use it willingly as well as unwillingly in order to safeguard their positions. These people are never the leaders in a group, and they usually never get to be the dominate one. They play both sides and when the conflict gets reconciled they'll usually get left behind.

Watch for those people who take more than they give. You can usually tell who the leeches are in a group. They're always the ones looking to further their own agenda at the expense of others or even at the expense of their friendships. Sometimes they may even mask it in some form of a trade in which they'll help you with something small and then end up asking for something big in return. It's the little ways they'll behave when it's something for them to gain or win. These people usually use others to climb up the ladder. Don't allow yourself to be the ladder they use to climb, they won't reach or look back down once they're up. You'll encounter these types of people the most in the workplace. They're the same people who take credit for the work or ideas they didn't have. The goal is to read these kinds of people from the beginning and only befriend those who act in your best interest or the best interest of the business.

Keep a watchful eye for those who don't clap or celebrate when you win. These are actual haters in the flesh disguised as your friends. Instead of being genuinely happy for you, they're actually jealous of your success when you achieve something. Personal success allows you to carefully analyze how other people behave toward you. It will expose people for who they really are. After reading my books and applying the necessary changes to your life, you're subject to come into financial success in the near future and your relationships may suffer because of it.

A fake friend won't stand up for you. Being that humans are social characters, there always seems to be some tension in social environments. This is one of the reasons we have friends in the first place. It's easier and safer to go out into the world together than alone. The belief that you have someone else's back and they have yours is the foundation for most societies and how they have been built. That's why betrayal of this sort cuts so deep and hurts so much. It's not that your friend didn't intervene when someone was talking bad about you, or jump in when a few guys where picking on you, they betrayed the bond you thought the two of you had with their harshness. A real friend will take personal damage to protect the bond they value in a friendship.

You may be friends because you have a similar objective instead of similar mindsets. This happens when the circumstances dictate for people go through a challenge or a prolonged period of time together. This is typical with friendships built in high school or during childhood. In the moment you'll believe that friendship will last forever, but people change and grow. Once the circumstances change and you have other options not forced upon you by the environment, some friendship will die because they weren't built to last. People behave like friends when it's easier to overcome a challenge together than alone, but don't confuse this type of social partnership with true friendship.

Watch out for those who ridicule you in front of others to make themselves look better. If you're the laughing stock of the group, then you're probably in the wrong group and around the wrong people. This is an interesting way to look at the relationships you have, because real friends make fun of each other all the time but it's the fascinating approach they go about doing it. On the other side of the coin, you'll find people who would never miss the chance to ridicule their so-called friends, especially if it makes them look better in eyes of someone new.

Another sign to look out for is if you notice that you only have frivolous conversations with someone. Trust comes from being vulnerable in front of someone else and for them to avoid taking advantage of the situation. Instead, they respond by bringing up their own vulnerability for you to see. That way both parties commit to supporting each other's best interests and behave as a group. This is one of the earlier traits of building a bond. If the relationship evolves to a point at which this type of support could be put into place, you could build something that could last. Fake friendships lack support of this nature, they gravitate around a shallow reality, and there's always this cloud that blocks you from knowing who this person really is.

A fake friend would leave you behind if something better comes along. Another sign that you're dealing with someone whose intentions are not genuine is that they would gladly trade in your relationship for another if they saw something to gain from it. Always be careful and weary of people who are leap frogging from friendship to friendship. In order for them to discard their current position they will never build a solid relationship. They have no anchors, and its best not to expose your vulnerability in front of them because they'll most likely use it to manipulate their way into a new group. Once you start to understand how other people think, it's almost like a superpower.

Unless you make plans and organize everything you never hang out. This speaks volumes to friendship dynamics and how valuable these relationships are to various friends in your group. Think about the last time you and your friends hung out. Who had to organize everything and pull everyone together? If it was you who did all the organizing, when was the last time someone in your circle did it? In an idea circle everyone in the group would see the value in their lives and look for ways to facilitate its development.

I mentioned earlier that presenting your vulnerability helps to establish trust. A fake friend will spill all of your secrets. A clear sign that someone isn't a true friend and isn't someone they portray themselves to be is when that trust is broken. Fake friends do not value your relationship, so they don't care if you get hurt in the process. They might even excuse their behavior as a slip of the tongue, but you can be assured it was more planned than they admit. So be sure who you confess or open up to.

Stay on alert for those who are tempting you with a bad habit. Let's say for instance, you just quit smoking or started a new diet to improve your health. A true friend would be more than happy to support you in your journey, and may even offer to join you. Always be careful of the person who's offering you a cigarette when they know you recently, or are trying, to quit. These people don't want you to succeed, because they themselves couldn't move beyond their current position. So the more people they keep at their level, the better they feel about themselves. Your success would only threaten their position, so they would only try to sabotage your attempts at trying to be better than they are.

Sometimes your inner circle or those closest to you would flat out tell you a particular individual is a fake friend. Sometimes you can be in so over your head that you fail to see the big picture. That's when you should rely on those who only want what's best for you. The unpopular version here will be your family. Despite the fact that you may not be seeing it or feeling it most of the time, they really do care about you and are not so emotionally involved in your outside relationship with friends to call it how

114

they see it. They often are able to tell when someone isn't being a friend for the right reasons. The second option is to run it by someone who has already proven to be honest and trustworthy.

Then you've got those who ask for help, but never offer it. They want you to be available for them but somehow they're never available for you. They only call when they need something, but when you need something from them they don't find themselves in a position to help. To simply put it, they are fake friends. In any real relationship there are unspoken rules about balance and equal offerings, when effort is rewarded by a similar type of effort. Judge people based on their effort, not based on their intent. I recommend you reward and keep close to you all those people who are putting in an effort to see you become a better person. If you've been having issues with friendships and feel like life in general isn't the way it should be, it's because it isn't. Reanalyze, reevaluate, and make the right decision. Always remember your gut instincts won't lie to you, but your mind and your heart will.

You may have friends but feel like you don't. This is a major sign that something is not right in your life. Despite what the environment is telling you, you feel the truth and there's no way around it. This is a weird place to find yourself in, and you can either start investing more time into your current relationships, or cut them loose and figure out how to build new ones. The last thing you want to do is find yourself being around people who don't care for your well-being, who don't want you to succeed or do better. Take my word for it, trust me on this and shake your fake friends.

No one is perfect, and that's completely natural. In addition to being self-interested, fake people are inauthentic. What's on the outside doesn't match the inside. These individuals are often so busy trying to make themselves look good to others that they don't even realize they've developed behaviors or attitudes that are not compatible with who they really are. Just like with everything else, the truth eventually comes out. Getting evolved with fake people can end in disappointment, so keep an eye out for these signs of a fake person.

People who are attention seekers and people pleasers are often full of insincere compliments, and they have no problem faking interest in you in order to win you over. Their desire to be liked fuels the bulk of their actions, so they pretend to like all the same things you like just so they can be included.

Some people are big on bragging about themselves. Phony people love to brag about themselves. Once they think they've got you hooked, they won't stop talking themselves up. This is likely because they want to impress you. Phony people are usually phonies because they're insecure. To hide that, they boast, show off, name drop, and go on and on about their talents and everything else they're good at. They're never at a loss for stories to show you how great they are. People like this are self-absorbed, and it'll soon become evident that they aren't concerned about you at all.

Their body language doesn't match their words. A fake person may fake wanting to know or learn about something or someone. If you're ever in doubt about whether to believe what they say versus what you see, ask them a question that would make them repeat something you previously said and test to see if their attention was truly in the initial conversation. Fake people exaggerate and lie. You know those people who always have to one up others? If you get a promotion, coincidently they just got a promotion and are expecting to get another one approaching the end of the year. If you're earning $20 an hour, they're getting

$25. They always have to be better than you. If you are attentive enough, you will probably catch a fake person in a lie within the first few minutes of meeting them.

They'll leave your side as soon as they recognize someone else. Fake people often use others to comfort themselves. For an example, if you were in a group setting and they didn't know anyone in the group a fake person would latch on to you just to appear to have friends or to seem popular. Then when someone more important arrives, they're off to latch onto them instead.

They are poor listeners. They need to be the center of attention, so they don't have time to listen and converse with you. Authentic people engage in two-way communication. They ask questions because they genuinely want to know the answers. Fake people on the other hand ask for the sake of asking. They're generally uninterested in whatever your response is, so they rarely recall things you've said.

Then you've got those people who are all about convenience. They get to dictate when you'll meet, where you'll meet, what you'll do, and it'll all be what's most convenient for them. Unfortunately, they regard you as nothing more than a tool to help them get what they want. They have no desire to be your genuine friend, all they care about is what you can do for them. They may agree to something or offer you assistance, but they won't actually be there unless they're going to benefit from the situation.

Fake people aren't the type of people you want to get too invested in, but watch out because they are everywhere. Their behavior is usually the result of some childhood or other trauma that has caused them to develop a defense mechanism to protect themselves. They might have been neglected in the past and

117

think that no one would look out for them, so they have to do it themselves in less-than-desirable ways. Deep down they fear that they won't have real relationships, so they use people to get what they want before they get hurt. Pay close enough attention, and you can spot a fake person from a mile away. Other times it's not so easy, but be careful when you start to see these signs. You don't want to let just anyone into your inner circle, and fake people are ones you definitely want to keep out.

CHAPTER 11

Knowledge of Keeping it Real

"Honesty is a very expensive gift; Don't expect it from cheap people."
—Warren Buffett

Since I covered the importance of identifying and shaking the fakes, I feel it's only right that I follow up with the equally important act of keeping it real and the overall impact of honesty. Honesty can seem like a simple word that should make sense to everybody. Ironically, though being truthful can at times seem so difficult. What I noticed throughout my years of living and my various experiences is that honesty can mean different things to different people. I grew up believing that people lie when they are ashamed or afraid of something. I believed that anyone who stands firm on a certain belief system, lifestyle, protocol, or code of conduct shouldn't have to lie about anything. I'm just saying, why should or would you? But then you have those people who would prefer a beautiful lie over the ugly truth—those who believe being slightly dishonest would seem appropriate. When you really think about it, there are different levels to honesty— from white lies to flat out deception. In this chapter I'm going explain "keeping it real" and the importance of being honest not only to others but more importantly to yourself. I mean, we are focusing on you being the greatest you, right?

Keeping it real, as the term is usually expressed, is all about being honest, and honesty is about being truthful. Simply put, it's about telling the truth at all times. When you hear the expression honesty is the best policy, it's stating that you should be honest and truthful as much as you possibly can throughout everything you do. When you're honest people are more likely to trust and listen to you. One fact of the matter is, since we live in a world driven by illusion of materialistic possessions and financial influence most people aren't even honest with themselves, so how can they be honest with you.

Now let's think about the times when you've stuffed yourself into that outfit you knew you couldn't fit into anymore, or strapped on a body-shaping suit and sucked in your stomach before the picture just to look the part. You went out and entertained your date that night in your spouse's car, fronting like it was yours. You may have had the times when your feet were aching in pain, but you kept the shoes on to keep up appearances. You may have had one too many shots at the club but kept on drinking so as not to disappoint your friends. Or you know your current relationship is toxic yet you stay in that situationship so you will not be looked at by your friends or family like you can't keep or maintain a successful relationship. These are just a few examples of lying, and believe it or not research has proven how much of being honest and keeping it real can improve your health. Telling the truth will help you sleep better, cause less tension, have fewer headaches and less anxiety, and improve relationships. You will be happier and far less stressed when you choose not to endure physical or emotional pain in order to look a certain way to other people, especially when you said you don't care what people think.

To be able to be truthful, honest, and possess the ability of keeping it real, you must first learn how to keep it real with yourself. To be truthful to yourself is not an easy thing, because there is a lifetime of buildups, of the habit of bullshitting yourself as well as others around you. Not to mention those people who encouraged, sponsored, and endorsed that this BS behavior from you is acceptable all this time. The problem with that is your life becomes the lie and you're stuck with living up to and maintaining this Cinderella lifestyle you created. There are a whole lot of people living like this. It goes back to the old saying, "Keeping up with the Joneses." This typically will go on until the life catches up with them, someone exposes them, or they simply hit a road block and re-boot themselves by starting over. To become 100% straight with yourself, it'll take a certain amount of appeal. If you do this one thing, this piece of life will work 100% for sure, and figuring out things will be a whole lot easier. When you learn and accept to be truthful with yourself, everything else becomes much simpler.

In order to find your way through all of that, you need to build a relationship with something sincere and heartfelt, What could be more sincere or heartfelt than the truth and complete honesty? When you express and expect nothing less than the truth, you find the meaning that sustains you in life, and you find the design of action that justifies the world. It's been said that you can tell much about an individual's character by how much truth he or she could take, which I find very interesting. Then you hear there's this idea from the old ways of civilization that the truth is the way and the path of life, and that no one knows themselves until they know their truths. I believe that to be true, because I don't think you can manifest who you're meant to be or who you are without knowing the truths of who you are or who you were. I think that it's literally in every aspect of the topic that the pathway to whom you could be is if you are who you completely are through your truth, further proving that the truth does set you free. Simultaneously it can destroy everything that isn't worthy of you as it does set you free. Every now and then life takes you through something that will straighten you out, and a lot of the old you burns away from the lessons of that experience. All of those character flaws and self-conscious traits then become ways of the past.

I think that honesty is the only real natural characteristic resource outside of mistakes. Being honest is the basis of wealth because when you treat people honestly, you usually receive honesty in return, and you can take people at their word and cooperate accordingly, resulting good business relationships. If you can't trust someone that you're confiding in, doing business with, or putting your life on the line for, then god only knows what that person is up to. An untrustworthy person is so complicated that you wouldn't feel comfortable doing anything that would otherwise seem simple, direct, and straight forward together. While trying to achieve a goal, you're going to be too busy trying to figure out what's really going on with that person. This in some form or fashion is partly why the world has so much corruption and is driven by many unethical activities.

We as human beings need honesty like we need food, and we are starving for the truth. In this age of Facebook, Snapchat, Twitter, and Instagram, too many people are so concerned with what others like, think, or say about them that their lives are driven by clicks of views and likes. There is so much deceit going on throughout social media that it's hard to detect fact from fiction, especially when the latter is so glamorized. I see so many people post like they have an abundance of money when they're actually failing at an alarming rate, and just terrible as parents. They may post different version of their meaning of success, when they're really lonely and miserable. I'll see posts of them in high-end designer fashions and I know that their living situations aren't adequate. What they don't post is the facts of their realities. But then again who really wants to post that they live at home with their parents, or haven't seen, spoken, or bought anything for their kids in quite some time with that flash money. They don't want you to know the truth about their lives, because that wouldn't be appealing to the image they're trying to portray. Now don't get me wrong, some people do honestly have it like that and it could be motivationally inspiring to like-minded individuals. However, if they're not true then these events or actions are considered deceitful and you're being deceived. If you're being deceived, you're being misled and lied to and that's far from keeping it real.

The power of honesty is that you become aware that you are consistently compatible with what you believe. Like the times when you say you're happy to be somewhere or to be doing something when in fact you're not. You can be pretending over something really small or to protect someone else's feelings, but to give it to you straight all of this pretending is also a form of lying. Now lying can be the most stressful thing you can do to your brain, because you usually have to follow up or support it with another lie, not to mention the burden of remembering the lie for future reference. A lie detector test solely depends on this stress of your brain and how it affects your body to detect lies. For instance, when you're hooked up to a polygraph machine, it can't tell if you're lying or not. It detects the unconscious stress levels and fear the lies do to your body. When you're hooked up to the machine it's able to detect the changes in electrical currents as well as the moisture coming from your skin, your body temperature, your respiration, your heartbeat, and even the pitch of your voice when you're lying. So you're literally telling on yourself.

There is a big difference between always living your truth and speaking your truth. You may be put in a situation in which

123

a friend asks you if they look fat. Instead of saying what's on your mind you can turn it around and ask them simply what they are thinking at the moment. This will allow you to invite them to share some of their truths. Unfortunately, there will be times when you may need to speak your truth or keep it real, so to speak, and others may not like it. People will often get angry, very frustrated, or just disappointed when you don't agree with their expectations or when you're not who they want you to be. Other times people can become uncomfortable, confused, or frightened by your truths, especially when your truths go against the established social norm. When keeping it real, there's going to be times when you have to face that discomfort, but usually what happens is something different and much better than making others angry. Usually, when you show people who you really are and speak your truths, you allow others to know the real you and not a façade of the real you. They get to see, know, and appreciate the real you for exactly who you are and keep it real with you in return.

When I used to look at the word honesty I would always think in terms of others and never myself. Honesty means truth, and truth is one of your most powerful allies. Once you are really honest with yourself about who you really are things will start to change very quickly, and you can evolve in amazing ways. We often avoid honesty because we're fearful that our truth would possibly scare or offend others. But if your truth frightens those around you, surly they shouldn't be in your circle. Doesn't it make sense that we would surround ourselves with people who would accept us in our brightest or darkest truths?

This doesn't necessarily mean to spill all of your secrets to everyone you meet. But rather to speak up about the things that are important to you and that makes up who you are. Nobody has the right to judge you. Judgment is reserved for the unawake and unconscious. Do not be ashamed of who you are, because nobody worth your time will be.

The only real shame will be to deny your true self. A life full of truth and honesty is a life of absolute freedom—a boundless experience of ease, peace, and prosperity. Living in fear is the worse way to live—period. The more truthful you are, the less fear you'll experience. It's strange how much we seem to fear judgment. But what is judgment other than someone's opinion, who sees themselves higher up than you.

If you knew with absolute certainty that nobody will ever judge you, how would you act? To release yourself from the judgment of others you have to do the same for yourself. Be honest with yourself about everything and you would quickly discover who you really are. You would realize that your truth is nothing to be scared of and something to be celebrated. It would bring you endless freedom and authenticity which, in my opinion, are two treasures of life. Saying yes to others just to please them while going against your own boundaries, beliefs, and morals can lead to all manner of chaos, not to mention you'd never live the life meant for you. I'm going to tell you something you probably should know, if you don't want to do something, don't do it. As simple as that sounds, remember that it will save you from a variety of disasters time and time again. No matter who is asking or what the situation is, if you really don't want to go along with something you don't have to do it no matter what. Never sacrifice your well-being for others. Of course this is different between this and stepping outside of your comfort zone, which is an awesome opportunity for growth. However, doing something that goes against your integrity will inevitably end in dysfunction.

Say no and don't cave into pressure, because it is your decision and no one else's. The same goes for the other way around. If you really want to do something, be honest and say so—be honest with yourself and do it. Holding back would only waste your time and make you wish you had done it earlier in your life (which is a form of regret). You have to be honest about what you want, and go for it.

So keep it real with yourself about everything. Keep it real with others when it comes to what's important and truly matters to you. Things will become clear and you will be on the fast track to a life you really want.

Since we as humans are tribal people, we can be very clannish and our natural senses aim to keep us around our own kind. It's because of that, acceptance can feel like everything and for some people acceptance is everything—it's their means of survival. I'm just only trying to get to whom this may apply to that the reality of how showing your false selves are holding you back. Of how that façade you're putting on will hold you back from who you can become, the life you deserve, and blessing you may receive. This business of telling the truth can take a lot of courage—it is not for the timid. It's daring to show your truth and keep it real at all times with other people. Without your truth and honesty, you will never know the limitless scope of your own natural talents and potential. It takes extreme bravery, and yet it's what you must do and who you must be to live your best life in the sponsorship of you being the greatest you.

CHAPTER 12

The Importance of a Code of Conduct and a Great Disposition

"Raking is easy, but all you get is leaves while digging is hard, but you might find diamonds."
—John Piper

In order to be the greatest you, you must have a strict way of conducting yourself, as well as a sound sense of a disposition that you live and stand by. The making of the two is not so easy to obtain as they come with a variety of elements to complete themselves in their entirety. In order to establish a code of conduct that governs your decisions and a disposition that enables you to respond accordingly, rather than to react inappropriately, you must obtain the following ingredients and live by them every day. I believe these ingredients are a combination of: morals, values, ethics, integrity, and principles. In this chapter I'm going to delve into the making and developing of each ingredient and discuss their importance in the role of you becoming the greatest you.

Let's look at the meaning and making of morals. Now if I steal from the rich and give to the poor, is that a good or bad thing? If my girlfriend is giving birth to my child in a vehicle, am I wrong for driving over the speed limit and violating traffic signals to get them to a hospital? What's good and what's bad? What is morality and ask yourself do you, as an individual have morals? If so, what are they? By Google's definition it means, "A person's standards of behavior or beliefs according to what is and is not acceptable for them to do." Morality is what society treats as right and acceptable. It's the unwritten standards of thoughts, behaviors, and actions everyone agrees to follow in an attempt to live peacefully. As you evolve, grow, and learn new things your morality will change. This is why morality couldn't be considered stagnant. It would naturally evolve with time as you encounter different experiences and beliefs within the world. Think about pre-marital sex, same-sex relationships, abortions, and the use of marijuana. All of these at one time or another would have been considered immoral practices long ago. But today, society has begun to accept all of these as moral. Since then you've learned to become tolerant of people regardless of their personal beliefs or preferences, and with this your sense of morality may have been compromised in the process. While everyone may not agree to all of these things nor practice them personally, things seemed to have flipped and it's now considered immoral to criticize the people who choose to live these lifestyles. Funny how that worked, right? You see morality is not just critical analysis, morality is intertwined with emotion. Attachments between parents, children, partners, and friends are the foundation on which morality stands. When you take away your emotions, all you're left with is critical analysis and decision-making based on cost and reward, but these aren't considered morals. Morality is a function of the brain that can be both biological and cultural. Biologically, what distinguishes us from other mammals is our ability to make moral judgments. This in itself is broken down into three things: (1) you being able to anticipate the consequences of your actions, (2) the fact that you can make valued judgments, and (3) you can choose alternative courses of actions. These three things work together to give you the ability to make moral decisions. However moral codes of conduct are strictly cultural, built on the need to cohabit successfully. That's exactly why every culture has its own sense of morality. Here lies the problem, because if your culture which is a particular nation of people, or social group defines what's moral or not, and you as an individual can't exercise your say in what is or isn't morally correct. Since we are focusing on being the greatest you, I'm encouraging you to follow that instinct or do what your gut tells you is right and wrong, what to do and what not to do, how to and how not how to do it, and not listen to a group of people being systematically controlled. I don't want to get to political (I'll save that for another book); however, I will say this—America was built on what was seen as moral, went against what was seen as moral and re-created what's considered moral, and then built a system that allows a minority group to live off the labor of a majority group.

While ethics and morals can be seen as one in the same, they are distinctively different. Ethics is basically the science behind morality. Ethics is the moral truth that governs a person's behavior or the conducting of an activity. It falls under the theory of taking the right action for the greater good, whereas morality is the practice of rightness or wrongness in your behavior. It's the branch of knowledge that asks the practical questions like "What should I do?" This leads to the study of things, such as merit, concepts, beliefs, or the norm. These are the things that shape our choices. Ethics asks you, "How should you live?" "What choices should you make?" "What makes your life worth living?" These questions require you to consider obligations to yourself as well as to others. They require decisions and actions and, in turn, these decisions and actions form a part of who you are or your character. It tries to help you figure out which available option is the best one. Just like morality, ethics could not be stagnant due to the fact that it lingers along the line of being happy and doing what's right. There are two ways of doing ethical investigations.

One seeks to set norms or standards that regulate right or wrong, or good and bad conduct, while the other aims to understand the nature and dynamics of the ethical concept and the way we learn and acquire moral beliefs. It's like one urges you to do good at all times while the other would question what is good. So it's important to have a sound sense of ethics because if not, your moral judgment will then be questioned and not by others but questioned by you. Ask yourself this—if you're not confident in the ability of your own actions or behaviors, how can anyone around you feel secure in your choices or decision-making? More importantly, how can you feel secure? You should always feel secure on what you believe is right and what's wrong. It all goes back to the old saying, "If you don't stand for something, you'll fall for anything."

So since you know that morals is the practice of ethics and ethics is the science of morals, lets delve into principles, which are basic truths that serve as the base for beliefs or behaviors and reasonings. Now, what if you can take chance out of your life, and you can know with certainty that the decisions and choices you're making would give you the outcomes that you want. Well that's what standing on principles is about, and I'm going to discuss the importance of having them.

Okay, so let's use the law of gravity as an example of principle. Since gravity exists and operates in the world in which we all live, it's something you can relate to. It doesn't matter if you know about it or not, if you step off a cliff you're going to fall, right? If you drop something it's going to fall, it doesn't matter if you believe in it or not. So you don't necessarily know how it works and whether you believe in it or not, the principle of gravity still exists. Water will boil at a certain temperature and become steam. Water at a certain temperature will also

130

freeze. There are principles that I myself don't understand through lift and thrust that allows planes to fly, yet I still board my flight trusting that the plane will arrive and land safely at my destination. The reason we are able to fly is because we have gained knowledge of the principles that enable flight. So with that being said it's easy to understand that you live in a world operated by principles, and these same principles have changed the world in which you live. Understand that those principles exist, but there are other areas of our life in which those principles exist, and those areas are happiness, success, and relationships.

You have all kinds of beliefs that you have accepted or developed throughout your life that may or may not be true. But if you believe something that's not in alignment or that's in violation of your principles, you're not going to get the outcome you may be looking for or expect. For example, if you believe your happiness is dependent upon someone else's, or that your happiness is dependent on a certain situation or circumstance, you'll never be in control of the happiness in your life, because you don't control your circumstances and you don't control other people. If you believe that happiness is a result of you being able to control other people, you're not going to be happy. That would be considered a violation of principles. You cannot control anyone other than yourself. You can only control three things and those are your emotions, your behavior, and your conscious thoughts. If you believe that in order to be happy you need to be in control of everything in your life, you're never going to achieve happiness. Happiness comes from understanding the principle that you don't control other people and you don't control external things. You can change your thoughts to be in alignment with your principles when you come to understand that you only can control you. Then you can choose to be happy in any situation or circumstance, and look for reasons to create happiness rather than continuing to think about reasons to remain unhappy. So if you want to live in a life feeling like you have control and that you do have control, you need to understand that there are principles that do operate and do exist and work the same way all the time. If it were not governed by principles, life would be utter chaos and we as humanity would not be able to grow, learn, and progress through life. What I want you to do now is to take inventory of the areas in your life right now that you are unhappy with. Are you accomplishing all the things that you want to accomplish? If not, then you should know that there may be principles that you're either unaware of, or that you are aware of and you're not following. Once you start following them, you'll be able to achieve the things in life you want.

Now let's get into values, and the value of having values. Values are like an inner compass. They are what matter to you deep down in your heart. Values are the expressions that are defined by the person you want to be, the way you would like to treat yourself, the way you would like to treat others, and the things you may feel passionate about. Because they are what matter to you, there is no right or wrong values. Values are a combination of principles, standards, convictions, and beliefs that you adopt as guidelines in your daily activities. They are a set of consistent measures and behaviors that you choose to practice in the pursuit of doing what's right and what's expected of you by society. Characteristics of values are learned early in life through family and friends. They can be specific, they can change from culture to culture, they can conflict between person to person, and they are often emotionally inspired. It's very important to know your personal values. Personal values are reflections of your needs, desires, and what you care about

132

most in life. Values are a great persistent force for your identity and can be thought of as decision-making guidelines that help you connect to your true self.

In developing or coming to know your values, you can ask yourself questions like, "What's really important to me, not only in a relationship but to me in general?" "What matters most to me?" "What's absolutely not negotiable?" There are plenty more questions to ask; however, I just wanted to name a few to kick-start your engine.

It's rumored, that values are typically acquired by the age of five, but I beg to differ because values are instilled in you through various experiences and what you've been exposed to in your life. It's not only what you say, it's not what you talk about, and it's not what you preach. Values are actually what you practice, and what you do with them will lead you to serve as a pillar to the world and helps you make worldly decisions. You need to recognize your values, you need to name them, you need to understand and define them. You need to think about them, otherwise you'll be walking around blindfolded. Secondly, you need to critically evaluate and analyze your values, because if you are one who believes values are instilled in you when you were a child, it might be because someone told you or demonstrated for you how to do the right thing. Also think about the cause and effect of that particular influence. Next, it's important to connect and associate yourself with others who share your values. In choosing your life partners and friends, this is vitally important. It will help you to find common understanding and agreement, and it can help you realize when things are not functioning in alignment with your principles. Finally, you should set life rules according to your values but not according to everyone else's. But if you don't know what your life values are, then how will

133

you be able to do this? Sometimes it's easier to know what you don't want than to know what you do want. So if you're still not sure what your values are, just think about the last time you were extremely annoyed. That situation that made you lose your temper, and what it was that caused it. For example, if one of your values is truth, it was very likely when someone was lying to you and you realized it. Similarly so, if you have respect as one of your values and someone is treating you disrespectfully, you're very likely to feel disappointed, angry, or possibly very sad, depending on your relationship with this person. So what I'm saying is, if you don't know what you want, try to figure out what drives you nuts, what makes you feel really uncomfortable, and work with those emotions to work your way back to what your true values are. Now if values are your inner compass, what good is it if you don't know how to realize it, read it, and utilize it to navigate your journey in life? It's for this reason you must come to terms with your own values.

You need to design, create, and develop your own core values in order to be able to lift "the greatest weight." "The greatest weight" is a metaphorical statement I use that represents the feeling that crushes you into repeating past mistakes, because of the unevaluated values you adopted from the world or your peers. The goal of this concept is to make you ask yourself, "Is what I'm doing truly meaningful, or am I just acting out in a way that my peer group thinks is right?" If you think that the things you are doing are worth repeating eternally, that you can be sure you are fully individuated, you will have enough courage and strength to lift "the greatest weight." If you don't think that the way you have been living is worth repeating innumerably, chances are, you haven't formed your own values and you are still a slave to your society and, even worse, to yourself. If you find yourself repeating the same mistakes you have always made and are left feeling crushed, chances are you haven't re-evaluated the morals imposed upon you by your peer group. Thus you are not a fully developed individual yet. Once you re-evaluate your moral landscape, only then can "the greatest weight" be lifted.

How many times have you found yourself turning a blind eye to somebody gaslighting or manipulating you, just because you didn't want to confront someone about something? Or how many times have you heard your friends or yourself say, "I always end up in a relationship with the identical person, with identical problems." If you were your own being with your own set of values, you wouldn't find yourself staying in toxic relationships because "It's the right thing to do." You would know that it's just you trying to be a good person by society's standards and, to be frank with you, that's just not worth it! In every situation ask yourself, "Do I desire this once more and innumerable times over?" If the answer is no, then you need to change yourself and re-evaluate your values, then and only then can "the greatest weight" be lifted.

True good lies beyond standard definitions of good and evil. Most of us live our lives in a self-imposed jail. Our jail cells are unemotionally determined by social beliefs that captivate the wildness and individualism of the human spirit. Many of us submit to the comfort of this cage. You can escape this enclosure of forced beliefs and awaken yourself to what you value personally. To break free and create your own values and meaning in life, you have to undergo this transformation, you have to go through this rebellious phase. You need to have the courage to break the chains of tradition, of beliefs, of society and perhaps you have to distance yourself from several people in your life. It doesn't need to be a violent and sudden reaction, it can and should be a smart, calm, but calculated definitive one. You can start by making a list of everything and everyone you think limits your freedom to be yourself. It can be an unfortunate unwritten rule at your work place, it could be your spouse who always tries to control and correct your behavior, or it may be your friends, or your parents who criticize you when you behave in a particular way.

Once you've done this try to think of positive strategies of how to change that situation. Maybe a brief discussion with your spouse in which you can address the issues, perhaps you talk to you colleagues or supervisors in a meeting at work regarding the problems you're experiencing, how it affects you, and how you would like it to change, or you could find new friends who appreciate you better. When you feel overtaken by "the greatest weight," you don't need to hide your aspirations, but instead you need to break from your self-made peer-based prison, and chase after the dreams that give meaning to your life.

I'm going to share this story that I recently came across. There was a founder and CEO of a successful corporation who for medical reasons was near retiring. But since he had no children of his own he had no one to claim as heir, thus having no one to leave the business to upon his exit. So one day he called for a mandatory meeting of all the staff members employed throughout the facility. In this meeting he announced that his health was weakening and that he would be retiring. Because of this he voiced his dire need to leave the company he so cared for in good hands. He went further to explain that the company should be left in the best hands he saw fit to continue his legacy, and that the person selected should be of high standards and top notch unquestionable character. He thought about asking everyone to write down the qualities they possessed, but he was sure they would write down only what they wanted him to hear. He instead gave everyone a seed with the instructions to plant, grow, and nurture a flower, and that he or she who returned with the biggest, healthiest flower would indeed care for his company the same as he did, and he would grant that person the position as the new CEO. All of the employees left that day with every intention of growing the healthiest and most beautiful flower. David, who worked in the mailroom and usually spent his days stocking shelves and organizing the company's incoming and outgoing mail, found himself spending day in and day out with his plant. He would water it consistently, give it the adequate sunlight needed and cared for it with over-extreme measures. I mean he would play music for it, and often on occasion he found himself even talking to it. But no matter what David did, he just couldn't get the flower to bloom and flourish. Nevertheless he refuse to give up. He continued caring for his plant up until the point of the deadline when all the employees would return back to work with the flowers that they were able to grow. So on this day, back in the meeting room the employees gathered around with extremely gorgeous plants and flowers, some small and some big, but all of them with something to show for their hard work and efforts. As David sat there with his flower pot full of dirt, he was laughed at and teased by all the other employees as he was sure not to get the position. He suffered the ridicule of his co-workers for about 10 minutes or so until the CEO walked in. The CEO carefully walked around the room examining everyone's plants and flowers with an observant eye. He admired a couple as he was sure to find the winner—the one person he would feel most suitable to lead and carry on his good name as well as his company's legacy. When he got around to David, he paused, he looked at the dirt-filled flower pot then back up at David with a confused expression on his face. David, feeling his boss's disappointment went on to explain all the love and care he put into the seed and the hardships he encountered in an attempt to get it to sprout, but to no avail. He felt he would never be successful at growing anything. After hearing enough, the CEO cut David off as he went to shake his hand. He told him that he shouldn't feel disappointed, that there was no need to explain, and how proud of him he was for participating in the challenge. He then raised David's hand as he shouted out, "Ladies and gentleman, we have a winner!" The CEO could tell by the baffled looks on employees faces that they were confused, so he explained, "I gave each and every one of you a dead seed, yet you all show up here today with these extravagant plants and flowers. In the event of my departure, this company shall be left in the care of the most fitting and honorable person I could find, and David here is the only one who displayed integrity. With that, it's my pleasure to introduce to you your new CEO." My first understanding with, and how integrity was defined to me was doing the right thing even when no one else is looking.

Do you always do what you say you are going to do? That is what often separates people who achieve their goals from those who don't. Integrity is the practice of being honest and showing consistent, uncompromising loyalty to strong morals, ethical principles, and values. Those who demonstrate integrity usually draw others to them, because they are trustworthy and dependable. It's not about proving to others that you do what you say but, more importantly, it's about yourself. You want to practice integrity because if your actions aren't aligned with your goals you won't achieve them. People fail at integrity because they accept everything that comes their way. Integrity is a necessary moral virtue and the foundation upon which good character is built. Acting with integrity means accepting understanding and choosing to live in accordance with one's principles, which would include honesty, fairness, and decency. You as a person with integrity will consistently display good character by remaining free of corruption and hypocrisy. Integrity is revealed when people act virtuously, regardless of circumstance or consequence. Now this often requires moral courage and, indeed, integrity is the critical connection between ethics and moral actions. *For what shall it profit a man, if he shall gain the whole world, and lose his own soul?* The first time I heard that it stuck with me forever, and it's in my wishes that it sticks with you as well.

CHAPTER 13

Knowledge of Accountability & Responsibilities

"If you fail to plan, you are planning to fail."
—Benjamin Franklin

Accountability vs. responsibility, do you know the difference? Well if not, proceed along and you'll learn the difference today. Accountability is defined as "an obligation or willingness to accept responsibility to account for one's actions." Responsibility is a duty or a task that you are required or expected to do. If you are responsible for something, then it's required or expected of you. The person who is held accountable is who is expecting you to do this task. Accountability is taking on a large overall challenge either through obligation, willingness, or sometimes both. If you are a business owner, you're going to be accountable for a lot, which is why you then need to dissect or divide the responsibility to the rest of your team.

As a business owner, manager, or team leader you may use the terms accountability and responsibility interchangeably, but actually there's a difference between the two. Throughout this chapter, I'm going to share with you one by one what the differences are. You may be wondering, "What do I need to know that for?" Well it's because if you get to know the differences between accountability and responsibility, you will become a better leader and, ultimately, a better person.

So what are the two major differences between accountability and responsibility? Accountability is about managing the outcome, managing the results, and the process in which the responsibility is about doing the task—doing the thing that's

140

needed. For example, you work in a store and you are in the customer service department. This particular department has different customer representatives. They might be responsible for picking up the phone, or handling on-line purchasing inquiries, or handling email inquiries to seal the deals. They typically interact with customers and consumers on a day-to-day basis, so they are responsible for handling the customer complaints, or handling the customer inquiries. On the other hand, the team leader or the supervisor of the customer service department is accountable. They are accountable for the results, for the process, they are accountable for making sure that everything runs smoothly in this department, they are accountable for everything—whether it's a good thing or a bad thing. Whether a customer praises you or whether the customer complains about you.

That's the first difference, the second difference between accountability and responsibility is that accountability typically goes to one person who is held accountable, and responsibility typically involves more than one person. Using the same example, an organization might have 10 customer service representatives, who are handling phone calls and talking to customers. All 10 representatives are responsible for doing the task of handling the customer inquiries but typically there's only one person, whether it's the team leader, head of the department, or supervisor who is held accountable—that's the difference. So more than one person can be responsible for doing the actual work, but one person is accountable for making sure the work is done right or to a satisfying standard.

So that brings me to this point, only one person can be held accountable for the incompletion of a task; however, many can be held responsible. Also you can be held accountable and responsible at the same time. But you may be wondering, why can only one person be held accountable? The answer to that is simple. If multiple people are accountable it leaves too much space for confusion, and the blame game of "you did this" and "you didn't do that," results in a lot of finger pointing. You should note that just because the CEO is generally accountable for the success of the business, it does not mean that he or she is accountable for everything.

Don't get me wrong, I do feel accountability is an active ingredient alongside the others in establishing and developing your code of conduct and possessing a great disposition. However, I want to elaborate a little more because it can sometimes conflict with being responsible and responsibilities. If you've ever heard or were taught that accountability necessitates personal responsibility, you'll learn that being accountable and being responsible are not the same thing. Let's think about it from different angles. The responsibility of a women who is pregnant is to eat properly to provide her fetus with a healthy diet. She should exercise a little, which may be walking or using an exercise bike, she should learn about the physical and emotional process of labor as well as giving birth, and she should take her prenatal vitamins as scheduled. But she isn't held accountable should she suffer a miscarriage, or if the baby is stillborn. These would be outcomes she shouldn't be held accountable for. The responsibility of someone who is diabetic is to make healthy eating and physical activity part of their daily routine, maintain a healthy weight, monitor their blood sugar level, and take insulin as recommended by their health care provider. Now as long as they're on top of their responsibilities, but suddenly they have a toe that needs to be amputated, you can't really hold them accountable. Here lies a couple of situations in which there's clearly a difference in being accountable and being responsible.

On your journey through life, you can only confront the problems that you are aware you have. Simply put, the only way that you can grow from your mistakes is to acknowledge their existence. Holding yourself accountable is a great way to begin that process, as it eliminates the time and effort spent on the unproductive behavior deviating you from your personal success. Accountability is a key element for personal achievement, because when you take responsibility for your actions you are then able to make the appropriate changes leading you to doing things differently. Holding yourself accountable helps you appreciate your own as well as the value of your peers. This is why knowing how to hold yourself accountable is such an important factor on your journey of you becoming the greatest you. Following are some steps to help keep yourself accountable.

For starters, accept when you may be wrong. Acceptance, according to human psychology is a person's ascent to the reality of a situation recognizing a process or condition without attempting to change or protest it. Often what we believe to be true and what is actually true are two very different things. Therefore to accept in this context is to understand that it's highly unlikely that you are always right all of the time. Not to mention the fact that sometimes without the intent we could be the cause of something, like hurt, blame, confusion, or conflicts. This acceptance will help you consider holding yourself accountable. Accept the positive as well as the negative, the milestones, and all of your failures.

To go with that, don't be hesitant or too prideful to straighten yourself out. When you can call yourself out on your own mishaps, those become moments of growth and maturity. What that does in return is to make you more mindful, and to consider different angles and sides to a story. It will allow a

143

deeper understanding of the problem at hand, because you may often view the story from your own personal perspective. Being aware that there are potentially many ways to view a situation opens your mind to understanding different point of views.

Often we avoid accountability because we don't want to be responsible for where that accountability could take us. We are often unsure of the reality of what awaits us on the other side of being held responsible, especially for something we may have neglected or gotten away with. This is why choice can be a perfect step in taking accountability for your choices. Choosing to progress is choosing to grow from the situation. This choice means to rise above from what has already happened and continue to mature despite what has happened. Choosing progress is making the choice to see past your own transgression and using those setbacks for growth. Always remember, the only way to move on is to move through what is blocking your path.

Some people see the things that they want, and some people see the thing that prevents them from getting the things that they want. You don't have to wait in line, you can do it the way everyone else has done it or you can do anything your own way. You can break the rules, but you can't get in the way of someone else getting what they want.

Sometimes you're every bit of the problem, and sometimes you're the only solution. Take accountability for your actions. You can take all the credit in the world for the things that you do right as long as you take full responsibility for the things that you do wrong. It must be balanced, because you can't have it one way and not the other. You get to take the credit when you also take accountability. It sounds easy, but it's not.

I don't know if you can relate or not, but I grew up with siblings and growing up we would do things to one another.

Usually when one got the best of the other, they would run and tell mom on that person. I remember one day my mom asking one of us, "Well what did you do to make your brother or sister do that?" Interestingly enough, that person would then become less telling on themselves and quickly redirect the blame on the other sibling. I've seen it all throughout school, in places of employment, and even hanging out being up to no good with companions or associates of mine. I'm not surprised that this occurrence would continue on all the way into my adulthood, and even into intimate relationships. This was all too familiar with me growing up, and I didn't know then that there was a word for it. That word is accountability. Being accountable is not just some word that you may hear being thrown around. Accountability comes with ownership and responsibility. It means to take responsibility of your choices and the consequences of those choices. As I researched this topic, I've come to realize that there are two aspects that come with being accountable— one inwardly and the other outwardly.

In the outwardly aspect of it, accountability is one tool for figuring out that if you do something outside your values, if you do something that's harmful to others or even yourself, what do you do about it? I like to break accountability down into three phases: (1) acknowledging your faults or the part you played, (2) making amends to whomever was hurt, and (3) learning from your choices in order to never make the same mistake twice. Obviously that includes understanding the impact that your choices have on you as well as others, and that people either in or out of your community were harmed. You need to understand all of the negative effects your actions had, and peel apart the layers of how and why you committed the harm in the way you did, or determine if you were just acting outside of your values.

145

Now the other aspect of accountability is inward, and that's more your personal actions or choices, for example, Jamie Foxx's song Blame It (On the Alcohol). What you need to do is to hold yourself accountable for consuming too much alcohol and allowing its effects to make the decisions instead of a sober you. Or when you made that conscious decision to go with your friends and hang out late into the night knowing you had work or school the following morning. Or when you knew that deadline was approaching, or that test was coming up, yet you neglected to accomplish your presentation or failed to study adequately to fully prepare yourself. We as adults know how sexually transmitted diseases are passed and the steps available to protect ourselves. But if you make the decision of not protecting yourself thus leaving you with an STD, you have no one to blame but yourself. When you are low on funds and find it that much more difficult to provide for your family, it's not your employer's fault—you agreed to work for those wages. You need to make your choices according to the earnings you make or need to make. Don't make excuses. Find a better job or add a side job to make ends meet. No one is to blame but you. This is about ownership—owning the part you play in the decisions you make, being accountable, and taking the necessary measures to right your wrongs. It's not the time to deny or ignore a situation assuming that somebody else is going to do it. You can't make excuses about why you can or can't do something. Constantly blaming somebody else and finger pointing when something goes wrong is no longer valid. No more sitting around and waiting for someone else to tell you what to do or how to do it. Don't use the excuse that nobody ever showed you, or that you were never trained. It's time for you to start taking the initiative. Google it, search on YouTube, or ask a friend. We're living in the technological age and the information is out there if you want it bad enough. You can't afford to just wait and see what happens. Remember, your situation won't change, especially if you don't change it. Just ask yourself, if not you then who is being accountable?

As far as responsibility, let me ask you if you have plans, dreams, goals, or aspirations that you're striving for or trying to live up to and, if so, what are they? Do you invite friends, family, mentors, or coaches into that and still find yourself stumbling over life's obstacles while attempting to achieve them? Well unfortunately, what you might be missing is not the plan itself but realizing the problem. Fortunately the problem is not as difficult to locate as you may think. Just go to the nearest mirror, take a long look at what stares back you, and you'll find the problem revealing itself in plain sight. What values, what principles, what standards do you strive to live up to, and what's important to you? How do you bring the, who (which is you, the problem) to the what (which is the goal, the accomplishment)? Do you count on your friends? Can you really blame your parents or mentor? Not at all, nor anyone else for that matter. If you notice when you stare at that mirror there's only one person in that reflection staring back and that's you. The excuses aren't there for anybody else, and the reason why is because you are the only one you have to blame for not being accountable for handling your responsibilities. You must take the responsibility to advocate for yourself because, if you don't, no one else is going to do it for you. You see, life is a battle and when you're in a battle field, you need to know who you are and whose responsibility it is to instill in yourself the attributes and qualities to win the battles life throws you.

In life, it's not the moments in these battles that define you, it's the choices and reactions that makes you who you are.

147

Within those choices resides your biggest potential, and it's called responsibility. Now just think about those moments in life for a second. Think about the times you were hurt, the times you failed, the times you made really bad decisions even when the decisions were not your fault. How many times have you looked back and blamed your parents for your bad reactions and bad decisions? How many times have you blamed your bosses or employers for the time you made bad career moves? How many times have you blamed your spouse or your co-workers for the choices you made? You don't want to be that person, and you don't have to be that person when you take responsibility for your actions and reactions. Challenge yourself to go a step further and instead of reacting simply respond. You can grow, thrive, and achieve when you take responsibility for the effect that you caused since every cause has an effect. Again the outcome is based on how you react and whether or not you responded accordingly. Bottom line is it's your responsibility to love yourself, know that you're enough, and that your decisions and choices are all on you.

Let's be honest, we all B.S ourselves in some way. That's just the reality of it; we all have our own excuses or reasons. We blame things on other people outside of our control sources of why certain things didn't happen. This story of why you weren't able to accomplish or become successful, and maybe your story sound like "Well I didn't have the same opportunities they had," or "I'm not as talented as you are," or "This happened because of that person, my boss did this, my co-workers did that, the school system, the justice system, the economy..."

We have these external things that we blame and excuses and reasons why we have done or not done something. The thing with that is every time you do that, every time you B.S yourself, blame others, or have a story, you're giving away your power, and you have no ability to change what your current circumstances are. You have no power to change your life, because you're putting it on something outside of yourself. You're putting it on something you have no control over. You have influence at best but you have no control over the outside world in any sort of way. But you have 100% control over yourself, over your own mind, over your own behaviors and actions in your life—you have full control over that. You might be influenced by the outside world, but you ultimately decide everything in your life, right? So you are responsible for everything in your life. Everything that happens to you in your life you are responsible for in some way.

Now you might not agree 100% with this and I get it, because it doesn't feel good to take responsibility in some cases. But I've come to understand that I'm responsible for everything in my life, and you are responsible for everything in your life as well. I'll give you an example of that. Let's just say hypothetically speaking that you were overweight. A lot of people would have a reason or some story as to why they're overweight. They might say, "Because I don't have the time to work out." They might say, "Because healthy food is really expensive, and I can't afford it." Or they might say, "Because of my genetics," etc.

Again every time that you're deflecting, every time that you're pointing the finger, you have no power to make change for yourself, but what it comes down to is you taking control over yourself. If you're failing in your life, it's because of you. The common denominator of people that fail is because of their choices and their excuses. It's not until you get to that point that you can put all those excuses to the side and say, "You know what? I am responsible in some way," and then you claim it.

That will give you back your power to change it, to do something about it to take the necessary actions to get out of that situation. To a certain extent, those stories may be true, but they aren't the reason your life is the way it is. Maybe it had an impact or some effect, but it's not the entire reason for your failures.

So getting to that truth, getting to the responsibility, and to that ownership is powerful. The thing is, most of us don't like to blame ourselves because it makes us feel like we're a failure and makes us feel like we're not enough. But again if you can get to that point and finally admit to yourself that you're that way because of your choices, then you can at least move in the right direction to make a change. You have to look at how you author and how you created events in your life. You need to be the one who accepts that you make or made decisions that led up to events occurring or outcomes arriving. That's why I say you're responsible for everything in your life. It can be challenging, and I get it, but if you can actually get to that point and claim responsibility and ownership for everything, you'll have control of your life and it will give you the ability to move forward and make the right decisions to change your life.

CHAPTER 14

The Must of Loyalty, Commitment & Dedication to Self

"Some people aren't loyal to you, they are loyal to their need of you...Once their needs change, so does their loyalty."
—Unknown

What's the true meaning of loyalty? If you look it up on Google or in the dictionary, the definition is the faithfulness of commitment to obligations, being faithful to someone or something else. Loyalty is an evolved human trait with both positive and negative features. The history of loyalty dates back to pre-biblical days, and in ancient expressions loyalty was giving your trust to an authority or an institution of some sort. In going back to the times of small tribes, as we evolved it was an evolutionary advantage for us to be loyal to our mates, loyal to our people, and loyal to our tribes. As time moved on, around the 1900s the definition of loyalty changed. It became manipulated into a devotion to a cause, and that's when the concept of loyalty was being leveraged to try and encourage actions from people who might not have acted on their own without the influence. Now there are debates and disagreements as to what kind of loyalty there is, such as friendship loyalty, national loyalty, social loyalty, political loyalty, and even loyalty within animals, for example, certain breeds of dogs are considered more loyal than others.

Since we touched a little on the history of loyalty, let's now discuss some of the benefits? For starters, loyalty can give constant support to a group or an individual. When you are loyal to a partner, you are more likely to stay together, start a close-knit family, and it helps with intimacy that could possibly lead to further conception. When you are loyal to your team, it helps with the fact that you can do more as a team than you can as an individual; however, it can have its ups and downs. But another element I'd like to introduce is when you are loyal to yourself. What about the part where you're loyal to your purpose and loyal to your aspirations? It's time that you dedicate and show loyalty to yourself, to your craft, to your creative talents, and to your future. You owe it to yourself and to those who depend on you to give your utmost and unquestionable loyalty to. Ask yourself, does the making of your life provide for you everything you want for your life? You have to feel that way, and if your surroundings aren't giving you what you need to feel that way, then you need to consider some changes and re-alignments. You need to be loyal to the betterment of your own behavior for the sake of your own best interest. It may seem a bit greedy and slightly narcissistic, but you can't provide for and be right by others if you can't provide and do right by yourself.

It's not until you do this that things truly change, and that progress is made at its highest level. You simply cannot tiptoe to success and you can't sneak up behind it, you have to own it. You have to go after what you want, knowing that abundance is your birthright. Your universe should revolve around making this happen. I have never in my years of existence seen a lion walk up to gazelle in hopes that it just falls over. The lion attacks it with everything that it has—speed, strength, tenacity, determination—and that's what brings home the prize. If you and your goals are not united, they are not the same, then that's a pretty good indicator that your loyalty is fighting the wrong fight. You should live and breathe your dreams, inhale, and exhale them. They should be at the forefront of your mind and should be the inspiration as you maneuver throughout your day. If you're not fully ready to commit your loyalty and dedication, then that should tell you your answer right out of the gate. You can complain about how many hours you've spent, cry about the aches and pains, and dwell on about your failures and shortcomings, but it's about you progressing, and if you don't immerse yourself in it, then none of that really matters. Be loyal to you and your cause, move how you need to move, and live how you want to live. Do what you must do to be what you must be to make your dreams real.

Loyalty also could be misconstrued about a bond between two people. I think loyalty should be turned inward to say, "I'm loyal to the core values and character traits that I want to live with and stand on." I feel that you have to decide who you are, and you have to decide what you stand for, and I think it's important that you're loyal to your values and stand by them no matter what somebody else does or says.

You've been loyal for years to people who aren't loyal to you. You've been loyal to a job that can care less about you, let alone your life. You're loyal to environments that been tearing your life apart. So the fact of the matter is you have been loyal to things that have been ruining your life. It's time to stop allowing that good heart to keep you in situations that aren't doing much for you.

Know that your kindness may be the cause of your minus, meaning that the good in you has prevented you from seeing the bad in this, the bad in that, and the bad in them. It's keeping you mentally, physically, and spiritually in places that aren't doing anything but adding more stress and hardship to your life. Think about what you're loyal to, you may very well be feeling empty

153

because you're being loyal to the people who are draining you. You're loyal to stress and anxiety, but cheating on your peace of mind. You're loyal to hurt and pain, but cheating on your happiness. You are being loyal to your current situation, and cheating on your destiny.

You're currently loyal to the things that bring you misery, and you're cheating on what brings you joy. If you continue in this behavior pattern, you're going to keep having low self-esteem, value others before yourself, and live life broken. You're destined to keep feeling empty because you're being loyal to things that bring no value to you, your current situation, or your life. With all this loyalty you possess, just imagine if you had it focused in the right direction. Just imagine if it was focused on your own purpose.

Stop putting all of your positive energy into these negative situations. Ask yourself how long your loyalty is going to belong to someone else before you give it to yourself. How long are you going to allow your loyalty to keep you in situations that may very well be ruining your life? You can be the perfect seed, but if you're planted in the wrong soil you'll never produce good fruit. What I'm saying is if you plant your seed into the wrong people, it won't produce prosperity, peace, or happiness. If you plant your kindness and good heart in the wrong environment, it'll never produce fulfillment in your life.

Give your loyalty to the people, places, and things that deserve it. Give your loyalty to the things that give it back. Don't allow your loyalty to turn your back on you, and don't be so loyal to others that you betray yourself. You can be so loyal to others that you're not even loyal to yourself. You're loyal to the promises you made to other people, but you can't be loyal to the promise that you made to yourself. That's not selfish, that's just becoming more self-aware. Just imagine how much better your life would be if you put your loyalty in the things that deserve it and into the things that appreciate it. How much peace would you have in your life? How much fulfillment would you have in your life? How much happiness would you have in your life? But what a lot of us are doing is spending our whole life chasing after something that wasn't meant for us to grasp in the first place.

Life isn't meant for you to be happy all the time. It's meant for you to go through things. It's meant for you to evolve as well as elevate yourself as a person. Bad things that happen in your life do not determine who you are, it's your reaction to those bad things that really make you who you are. Can you be relied upon in crises when things don't look good? Who are you inside? Yes there are things in life that'll bring you down. They may even have you stressed and little depressed, but don't let them keep you there. Those are the moments that make you who you really are. You have to see the life that you want. You have to believe that you can be something that you're not right now. You can be better and you can do better as long as you stay loyal to your cause.

Dedication is the quality of being committed to a task, to a person, or to a purpose. It's to have devotion, perseverance, and unquestionable loyalty. I want you to think about this, because you have those characteristics inside of you. You may be dedicated to Starbucks, social media, your career, or even your family. Take the time out to ask yourself, "What am I dedicated to?" If you really think about this dedication is easy when it comes to something that you love or want to do. But when it comes to something that you don't want to do, then being dedicated to it becomes extremely difficult.

Look at your life right now. Whatever you've done up to this point in time in your life is working. Whatever you have produced came out of you as the results of the kind of person that you have become, it's a result of your choices, it's a result of your consciousness. Now you have to ask yourself, "Am I satisfied with what I have produced?" Where you're at in life, ask yourself if this is what you want, or would you like things to be better than this? What happened to you being dedicated to your goals, wants, and desires?

What I'm saying here is learn to be your own energizer. Start building yourself up, start encouraging yourself, start saying to yourself, "I can do this. I can make this happen." Decision-making is the force that shapes destiny—personal, corporate, or business destiny. Think back to a decision you made years ago. Whether it was 5, 10, 15 years ago, you may not have realized it at the time, but that decision was one of the most important decisions of your life. Had you made a different decision or had you gone in a different direction, your life would be completely different today. The secret then is to get damn good at making more effective decisions. By the way, you're not going to always make the right decision, but most people don't have the guts to make the tough decisions because they want to make the right decision, so they make no decision which can be a bad decision. Then what happens is the world takes over for them. They become of the world, lost in the world. If you're dedicated to your vision and your purpose, every decision you choose would ultimately lead you to where or who you want to be. Being and staying dedicated to your decision-making is power.

Just working on your goals is not enough. If you want to become successful you have to become obsessed. Dedication is the quality of being dedicated, as well as being committed to a task or a goal. There are way too many people who casually approach their goals then become surprised when they never achieve them. If you are serious about your goals, then you have to become captivated in the many steps to achieve them, and that's when you will start to see real progress. For instance, I'm currently dedicated to completing this book, so that means less time spent watching or listening to podcast shows, and reading books from other authors. One thing that you'll have to become aware of is when you become dedicated to one thing, you'll have to give up other things temporarily. This is okay because the key word is "temporarily," and once your goals are achieved, then you move on to the next accomplishment, but you have to stay consistent if you want to achieve the results you desire.

I'm sure you already know that distractions can be a waste of a lot of your time, and dedication is a great way to avoid distractions. What I like to do is to become so busy and dedicated to my goals that I basically don't have time to waste time. It's that Bill Gates approach that says "Don't waste time to have time," and we all have time unless we waste it. Make sure that you don't work on multiple things at one time. Choose one thing, and dedicate your time and energy in achieving that goal. Remember, dedication is complete and wholehearted loyalty.

Commitment is the foundation of great accomplishments. Without commitment Tyler Perry, who went from homeless and sleeping in his car, wouldn't have been able to be a successful actor, comedian, filmmaker, and playwright. He created over 14 Madea films that generated millions of dollars, which allowed him to purchase his own studios to further produce films that have enabled him to have a net worth of a billion dollars by the age of 56. Without commitment we wouldn't be able to enjoy all those athletes that come together every four years, showing us both their mental and physical endurance at the highest level in Olympic competitions. Without commitment, we wouldn't be able to see an everlasting display of love from the likes of couples such as Barack and Michelle Obama, Denzel and Pauletta Washington, or Samuel L. Jackson and LaTanya Richardson Jackson, just to name a few. To achieve greatness in the areas that are important to you requires that you deeply invest yourself and commit, and as you do that it shapes a life for you. What you may have often overlooked though, is how all of your past commitments—whether they be big or small—contributed toward your current life.

One of the best pieces of advice that I can give you is, if you're going to commit, then commit. If you're going to commit to something most of the fear and most of the negative emotional response all come from what happens before you make the decision. Once you've made the decision most of the stuff that was worrying you tends to go away. So know that the decision has been made and all that's left is for you to deal with the circumstances as they present themselves. That's something that you can get busy with right away, rather than sitting back thinking about worse-case scenarios, and worrying about this or worrying about that.

Let's start with a small commitment that you make every day, and that's the simple commitment to get out of bed. There are those moments when you really don't want to get out of bed, but you know that if you're going to get anything accomplished you have to at least start with getting out of bed. You can't brush your teeth, take a shower, or get the kids ready without that first commitment. So while some acts of commitment are done automatically, some require a lot of thought and reflection, and I'm talking in particular about your life, work, and relationships.

Ultimately, you do get to choose. Each and every one of your commitments shapes your life—from the constructive to the destructive ones. From the ones you think about to ones you don't, from the big ones to the small ones—all of them impact your life in a different way. Ultimately, the power is yours, because it's you that gets to make the choice when you stop. Take a look at your life and ask, "Hey, what am I deeply committed to?" Keep in mind it's a difference between love and loyalty, and some people don't really love you, they love the benefit of being a friend of yours, so they act accordingly.

Don't cheat yourself. Don't allow people to lower the sticker price value of you. Understand that you're not for sale, you can't be bought. But when it comes to you your value is not negotiable. You don't settle for less, period. You can't because when you settle for less, you're teaching yourself that you're not enough. The more that you settle for less, the more you're programming yourself to tell yourself that this is what you deserve, and you start to live a life of settling for less because you allowed somebody for whatever reason to allow you to negotiate your work. Your values are your values, period! Stay committed to yourself, your work, your journey, and don't change it for anybody.

What I've come to learn is that in order to have or know a plan, you have to know what to commit to. That commitment isn't only a word, it's really a process, and sometimes you have to develop that plan in order to commit. Part of that plan could be the need for letting go of other commitments. Now as easy as that may sound, sometimes it can be extremely difficult, and you might ask, "How does a commitment differ from an obligation?" Well, for example, I was committed to the street life, and the rules of the underworld but obligated to my family. Commitment is the quality or ability to be dedicated to a cause or activity.

159

You may have heard in your life, or live by the terms you're either committed or you're not. But what I find interesting is, there levels of commitment. Some high, some low, some with every part of you invested, and some in which you're just partially invested. Because commitment can vary, the question becomes, "Is there a way you can create commitment within yourself to things that matter most and will shape your life in positive ways?" Also, "Are there ways you can learn to let go of commitments that are holding you back or are quite hurtful to you?" The answer is yes, especially when you look at commitment broken down into three elements with the first being pro's and con's. Take a second to analyze the pros and cons to what it is that you aim to invest your commitment.

The next would be contributions. What do you have to contribute toward this particular commitment, such as your time, energy, money, talent, creativity, love, or heart to open up and share who you are, and is it even worth it? The last would be choices. Always remember you have choices that can provide you with options. Although options tend to work against being committed to a one certain thing, they could also provide you with a means to utilize your skills elsewhere to re-align or shift your position in life, work, or a relationship. Fully commit to excellence, because until you do, you will be left only with a vision and a false sense of reality. You're a winner, and you don't have time to spare. Set your mind on your target and crush it. That is your only option.

CHAPTER 15

Knowledge of Fear and How to Deal With it

*"F-E-A-R has two meanings: Forget everything
and run, or face everything and rise.
The choice is yours."*

—Zig Ziglar

It's pretty clear that one of your many great hurdles is fear. Now it may be the fear of trying, fear of failing, fear of looking bad, fear of the unknown, or the fear of actually being successful. It's these fears that could be the main reason you prefer to live within your comfort zone. The good news is you can learn to beat fear. Each of us throughout our course of life must come face to face with our own fears and, at some point in time, confront them. Conquering your fears is a skill that anyone can develop. But the ways to do that might be quite different than you think.

I've heard people say that fear isn't real, and I say that's so not true! In fact, there are probably things that you are afraid of doing right now in your life, in your relationships, and at work. The fact that you're afraid is robbing you of all the experiences that you want to have in your life. For instance if you're afraid to fly, that fear will limit your ability to travel and see the world. Fear is here to stop us all from doing things, but that doesn't mean that it has to be. Fear is real, but I'm going to share with you a secret weapon that I have used for years to beat any sense of fear within me.

First, let's go over a few facts about fear. What it is, what it isn't, and some things that you may not know about fear. So fear is a physical state in your body that happens to be exactly the same as excitement. Yes, fear and excitement are the exact same physical state. Your heart races, you might sweat a little bit, you get butterflies in your stomach, and your body goes into this ultra-aware state as it gets ready for action. The only difference between fear and excitement is what your brain is doing as your body is all flustered.

When you're excited, your brain is thinking about how cool and fun skydiving or getting on that roller coaster is going to be. But when you're afraid, your brain is going "Uh yea, no, not I, I'm not going to be able to do it, this is dangerous, get out of there." It's saying something completely different. So what's critical about understanding this is that your mind is either working for you through excitement or against you through fear to your advantage.

It's been proven through research that when you try to ignore your fears, you're actually making them worse. Research on the subject has proven that positive thinking alone also can make your fears worse. So what do you do when you have to go talk to your boss about getting a raise? What do you do when you have to get on a plane when you're actually terrified of flying? What do you do when you have to give a presentation and you are afraid of public speaking? Here's what you're going to do.

You're going to use a strategy, the same one that reverses your fear and turns your fright into excitement. This is how you do it. You're going to use a five second rule in combination with what is called an "anchor thought," and that is going to reframe what your mind is doing. You are doing this so that your mind goes from feeling agitated, which is making you afraid, to reframing it from agitation to feeling excitement.

Excitement and fear are the exact same thing in your body, it's just what your brain calls it. When you start to sweat, when you start to have butterflies, and you get to feeling your heart race, tell yourself that you're excited. Say to yourself, "I'm excited. I'm just overly excited to get on this plane. I'm just excited to ride this roller coaster. I'm excited to get out there and talk in front of 5,000 people." What that does is send a message through your body telling your brain why you are agitated and excited. The mind's twist to this is that you may be feeling fear, but you told your brain it's just excitement, that way you won't feel afraid. Remember, excitement and fear are the exact same thing in your body. The only difference is what your brain calls it.

Now you may have a fear of flying, and I can relate because I know many of people who have never been on an airplane due to their fear of flying. If they can't get somewhere by bus, car, or train they aren't going. So first things first. If you have to do something that really makes you nervous or that you're afraid to do, before you're about to do it come up with an anchor thought.

What is an anchor thought, you ask? Well, an anchor thought is something that's going to anchor you so that you don't escalate the situation into a full-blown panic attack or a situation in which you screw things up. It's a way for you to anchor yourself so that you maintain control over what you're thinking and how you behave. It's important that you pick something that is in the proper context of what you're afraid to do. So with flying, pick an anchor thought that has to do with the trip that you're taking. For example, if I'm boarding a plane to fly back home to California, a anchor thought might be a picture in my mind of my mom and I attending a Warriors game. That's a thought that brings joy and excitement, while also being part of the trip that I'm taking.

If you're having a conversation you need to have with your boss, pick an anchor thought about how you'll feel after having that conversation. Maybe it's you picking up the phone and calling somebody that you love and telling them, "Oh my goodness, you won't believe this, it went so well." Or you walking out of the meeting with your chest poked out like "Yeah, I just survived that conversation, I feel pretty good about myself."

Now that you have your anchor thought, you're ready to beat the fear. So let's go back to the example about the plane and flying. You're on the plane flying to your destination; you catch a little turbulence, your body's going to start getting agitated, you're starting to get nervous, your heart starts racing. One of two things is going to happen, you can't control how your body may feel but you can always control what you're thinking about, and you can always control how you act. So when you're on that plane and the turbulence does hit, step one is to count down from five. This step is essential, because it allows you to switch gears in your mind, and it triggers your mind to let your brain know that you are now in control of your thoughts. You interrupted the fear factor, you've settled your thoughts, and now your brain is ready for that anchor thought.

So then what you do after you count down from five is to insert your anchor thought that you've already come up with before the flight. It can be anything. Mine may be chilling on the beach in Monterey or looking forward to a Warriors game with my mom. Yours can be whatever appeals to you. Then you start telling yourself that you're excited, so excited to get back to do this or can't wait to meet this person to do that. At this point something remarkable is going to happen in your brain. Because you've interrupted the fear, because you used the five second rule to assert control, and because you have an image that contextually makes sense in your brain that you're actually flying to wherever, and your brain registers the excitement and never senses the fear. It's that your body is in a state. Going back to the first thought, remember fear and excitement are the same thing. The difference between fear and excitement is what your brain is saying.

By using the five second rule and an anchor thought you can actually switch the gears in your mind and reframe the thoughts of fear into thoughts of excitement. Because you have a vision that makes sense based on what you're doing, your brain buys it. When you do it and it's done right, you can actually trick your brain. What I find most amazing about this is, if fear does stop you this will change your life.

Fear is real, you can't control your feelings that are going to rise up in your body when you are on an airplane or talking to your boss, or when you see someone who is attractive and you really want to go over and talk to that person. But you can always control what you think, and you can always make a decision about the actions you're going to take. So the next time you feel afraid, apply the five second rule, tell yourself that you're excited, and visualize what you're going to do once you reach your destination.

If we were to think about where fear comes from, you must first understand that it's wired in. It's actually a natural part in a region of your brain. Through research I've learned that it is called your amygdala. This part of your brain is there to keep you alive, and contributes to your survival instincts. One of the most common ways it helps to keep you alive is that it generates fear to steer you away from danger. It's the reason why you duck when you hear gun shots go of, or if you happen to be at a baseball game and the batter loses the bat while swinging at a pitch and you duck down to prevent from getting hit. Or when you were younger and that dog came charging at you, and you immediately ran incredibly fast without hesitation. This is the part of your brain that thinks, "That's a little too high, I'm not getting on that roller coaster." Or "Okay, I'm a tad bit too close, let me step back away from the edge of this cliff."

This part of our brain is great at its job; however, it's a bit of a glitch to the system. The glitch is, this part of our brain doesn't really know the difference between the good challenges and the dangerous ones in life. It's not familiar with the good and bad risks, so its tactic is avoiding risk altogether. There are four likely situations that create and enhance fear. Those are: uncertainty, attention, change, and struggle. The overall idea here is that if all four of these are present, then fear itself becomes present. I think you may agree with me that those four elements can describe a dangerous situation. But these same elements are present in the best learning opportunities as well. They are present when you perform for a show, being interviewed for a job, or competing against others in sports. What happens more times than others is when you feel fear you often find a way to avoid doing the whatever it is that prompted it, which is great when it comes to danger but not much when it comes to learning or growing.

While this kept me safe from being chased by dogs, it was also the reason why I never raised my hand during class to ask those questions. When I would think about raising my hand to ask a question, everyone's eyes would have been on me and this would have caused attention. Then I had in my head the uncertainty of whether I would be laughed at by the other kids for seeming slow and asking a stupid question. Through this unwanted attention and uncertainty, fear won the battle. This caused the fear from me raising my hand in class to waiting until the class was over to pull the teacher aside then ask my question.

It's for this same reason you can have a report due in two weeks but what usually happens is you wait until the last minute to do it. We've all been there, but the reason why is because procrastination in the same way comes from that amygdala part of your brain. Every day leading up to the due date you have a choice to either research or play video games, study, or watch television. Most of the times, you'd rather watch Netflix, the latest episode of your favorite show, or played on the PlayStation. To this part of the brain, the world is viewed as either black or white. It doesn't really know what we're doing and it sees that I can either struggle right now or not struggle, and it's always going to choose to not struggle. It's for this same reason you may tell yourself, "Next week I'm definitely going to start working out," but when the struggles of working out come, you find yourself falling back to your normal routine because it was less of a hassle. Or you might tell yourself that your New Year's resolution is to start a diet, and a week or two into the new year you're back to eating the same unhealthy foods. I want to be clear that the option of choosing easy over hard is the force that's driving a lot of your behavior. It's the force between a lot of your decisions.

What I'm getting at is the tactic of avoiding uncertainty, attention, struggle, and change is great if you're ever in danger, but most of your life is spent not really in danger. In this case that tactic could really rob you of many opportunities to grow. That leads me to ask you just that, "When has fear robbed you of an opportunity to grow?" Here's the truth about fear, it's hindering and it's robbing you of many great potential outcomes. Not only that, but it's also robbing you of something else equally important, and that's experience. Having that experience of going through the interview process, recording in the studio, singing on that stage, or approaching that person you find yourself attracted to is good for you whether you succeed or not. Every day of your life fear is robbing you from growing. It's really easy to sit in a comfortable room and read *Be The Greatest You,* and talk about what you should or shouldn't do, or even talk about what others should or shouldn't have done, but until you're in that person's shoes or sustain the lack of that person's experience, who's to say what the outcome may be. What we do know is, without the conquering of your fears whether they are big or small, who's to say what life-changing event could arrive from believing, betting, and taking a chance on yourself. You never know, you may like the life that decision affords you. Take a leap of faith in yourself!

I'll share a story with you on how fear impacted my life. I was continuing my education after high school and attending classes at Merritt College in Oakland, California. One day as I was walking into a class, this man that I had seen on campus a time or two was walking out. We caught eye contact and he stopped and asked me, "Excuse me, brother, how old are you?" Unsure of why he was asking me my age, I hesitantly said to him, "I'm 18, why?" He then said, "If you invest $100 in Yahoo, by the time you turn 25 you'll be a millionaire." Around that time I had a bunch of $100, so investing just one wouldn't have broken me, but it was the fear of the unknown mixed with the lack of educating myself on stocks and how to invest that prevented me from doing so. Needless to say, since then Yahoo stock soared through the roof, and Yahoo as a company became a success. While I was being fearful, I missed out on a life-changing investment. I'll give you another example, because I have so many missed opportunities that I can recall. The year was around 1999 or 2000. I was driving around with my then-girlfriend and I don't necessarily know how the topic came up, but I was attending a school called DeVry University. It was a school for business and technology, and I was learning about computers and how to program them, or something like that. So a topic came up and I was explaining to her my prediction of how computers and technology were going to pretty much take over the world. I was going to this school and juggling another type of lifestyle, but I was deterred from attending classes and giving my studies 100% in fear of how my peers would have possibly viewed me. Afraid of being looked at like a nerd, I wanted to uphold and maintain my little street thug image. Well as we all know, this world wouldn't be what it is today without the use of technology and computers, and since then technology as we know it has only enhanced and I don't see it slowing down any time soon. Had I stayed focused on my assertion of where the world was headed, I'd most likely been ahead of the dot com boom, but my wanting to participate in street life to uphold an image and my fear of being looked at like a nerd eventually led me to being confined in a prison cell the size of a closet with another man. I was shipped away from my family and incarcerated in the penitentiary system.

So if you happen to wonder how to kill off this kind of thinking, or how to conquer the part of the brain that promotes fear, the answer is simple—you must embrace it, you have to entertain and dance with it. If you're seeking to destroy, defeat, or conquer this part of your brain, you will fail. Your brain is nothing but electricity and chemicals, so when you push back against the amygdala part of the brain, it freaks out. That's how people suffer panic and anxiety attacks. Try to think of this part of your mind like that inner compass, and when it freaks out it may be telling you that you're on to something. You're about to do something that's brave, bold, and powerful, and you should listen to it by doing the complete opposite of what it wants you to do. When you find that your brain is telling you to stay in that comfort zone and you do the complete opposite, of course it's going to freak out. But the freaking out is a signal that you're in a learning experience once you understand how it works.

It wouldn't be mentally correct for me to encourage or tell you to have no fears and to become fearless, because it's impossible. That's not how the brain works, so that's something that can't be done. When doing something that involves uncertainty, attention, struggle, and change you're going to feel fear. The only way to not feel fear is to not do it, not care, or hold back, and that's not what you want. So logically if you care and it involves uncertainty, attention, struggle, or change you're going to feel fear. You can call it what you want but that feeling is still there. Then you have people who are going to be or are already in your ear telling you what you shouldn't feel and what you shouldn't fear. The problem with that is you may start to feel shame, because now you're thinking, "uh oh, I'm not supposed to feel like this. Something must be wrong. I must not be ready, because no one else feels like this," and all of those feelings will pile up and make the initial feeling of fear worse. But it's coming from this flawed idea that you're not supposed to feel fear. The message I'm trying to convey is for you to understand this feeling of fear before a big job interview, a performance, or a talk. Anything that stretches or challenges you doesn't necessarily mean something is wrong, it doesn't mean that you're not ready, it simply means you're a human being, and that's the human response.

Now in the process of going after that big bold dream of yours, there's one thing that stands in your way, and that's called fear. If your dreams don't scare you, then you're not dreaming big enough. When you attempt to go after something larger, you actually feel like failure is possible, and that's when you have to muscle up your courage to do it, afraid, ready, or not.

I'll confess that when I starting writing this chapter I began by using a very old approach to this topic due to how I was raised, my experiences, and what was instilled in me growing up. But I understand that would have been a very demanding, not to mention negative approach, mixed with what you can't or shouldn't do. With an upgraded approach, I realized that it's natural, and it's human. With the knowledge I've shared so far, you should understand how likely you are to be placed in those fearful situations, and do the things that will help you learn, grow, gain the experience, and get better. To be honest with you, topics that I covered so far made me reflect back at times in my own life and how fear played a major part of the many missed opportunities, missed fortunes, and possibilities I've encountered in my life. I think back at all the times I had felt I was either too young or wasn't smart enough to do what was in my mind to do. So I'm proposing that when you feel fear, use fear. Use it against itself to enable you to reach a higher plateau, to challenge yourself and become a greater you.

CHAPTER 16

Knowledge of
the Power of Words

"Sticks and stones may break my bones but words can never hurt me." Or could they?

All things are made and created through words, which are the cosmic sounds that fill our life and matter to us most. To understand how powerful words are you need to know what the term "word" means on an obscure level. You need to understand the standard definition and investigate other related words. In this chapter we will go over the power of words and how they impact our lives.

Words have the power to change the world. Words also have the power to unite or divide us. Words are sung, written, screamed, and felt. They overcome silence with a meaningful sound. They make you think, act, and even dream. They tell stories that may or may not ever happen. They promise things that may or may not ever come into fruition. Words are your voice and your power to change. They are triumph over the silent dullness of a joyless life. They are ideas and can be your greatest aspirations, because a single word is action that does matter.

A person who knows the power of words becomes very careful of their conversations. They have only to watch the reaction to their words to know that they do not return void. Through spoken words alone, humans are continually making and creating laws for civilization, society, and humankind. I once knew someone who said, "I always miss a car, it always seems to pull out as I arrive." His daughter would say, "I always catch a car. It's sure to come just as I get there." This had occurred for years, each one making a separate law for themselves—one of failure the other of success.

This is the psychology of superstitions. The horse shoes or the lucky rabbit foot contains no real true power, but spoken words and beliefs said it would bring you good luck, creates expectancy in the subconscious mind, and may attract a lucky situation. However, I find that this will not work when you have advanced spiritually and know a higher law. You cannot turn back, nor can you put away sculptured images. For example, I knew two people who had great success in their business for several months until suddenly everything went downhill. We all collectively went to analyze the situation, but I found that instead of making their affirmations and looking toward a higher spirit for success and prosperity, they had each brought these little objects in the shape of owls as lucky charms. As I noticed this, it came to my realization that they had been trusting in these lucky owls instead of their own abilities. After a brief discussion and a little convincing, they threw the owls down a laundry chute, got back to focusing on their brand, and shortly thereafter all went well again.

This doesn't mean, however, that you should throw away all of your lucky ornaments, or rabbit feet that you have laying around the house, but you must recognize that the power backing it is of a higher element. The object itself only gives you a feeling of expectancy. Owing to the vibratory power of words, whatever you voice you'll begin to attract. Those who continually speak of disease will always seem to attract it. After you know the truth, you can't be too careful of your words. For example, I have an old school acquaintance that from time to time would reach out and say, "Hey let's link up, throw some meat on the grill, pop a couple cold ones, kick our feet up, and talk about old times." The problem with that is my old times consisted of a lot of chaos, trauma, anxiety, stress, mayhem, and imprisonment. So rather than meeting up and discussing old times, I declined his offer but instead replied with, "No thank you, I've had enough experience of talks about old times in my life. They're too expensive, but I'll be glad to discuss new times, and talk about what we want and where we're going verses possessions we've had then lost, and were we've been."

There's an old saying that says, "Man only dares use his words for three purposes, and that's to heal, bless, or prosper." So just like what you do unto others, others will do to you; what you say of others will be said of you, and what you wish for others will be what you are wishing for yourself. Curses like chickens come home to roost, so if you wish bad luck upon someone, you are wishing bad luck onto yourself. If you wish to aid someone to success, you are wishing and aiding yourself to success.

Everything going on in your life is due to the words you either hear or say to yourself. It really makes no point in asking someone, "What's the matter with you?" We might as well say, "Who's the matter with you?" Your body can be renewed and transformed through the spoken word along with clear vision. Goodwill produces a great aura of protection over the one who sends it, and no weapon that is formed against him shall prosper. So, in other words, love and goodwill destroys the enemy within yourself, therefore you'll have no enemies on the external. There is peace on Earth for those who send goodwill to others.

I mentioned earlier that I had siblings in the households that I grew up in, and the fact that we often got into it with one another. Well, during the course of our many disagreements one may call another stupid and as soon as it was said my mom would be on top of it. I can hear my mom now as she would scream out loud "Don't you let me hear you say that ever again, ain't nobody stupid in this house." Of course we as little kids didn't understand the power of words and how effective they can be. It'll be times when I may get out of line or find myself in some type of trouble by doing whatever my young mind had driven me to do. If or when it had gotten back to my mom, she would check me on the spot and put me back in line quick. But while doing so, she may ask, "Who do you think you are?" I would reply by saying "nobody." She would then continue but every time I would say "I'm nobody," she would correct me by saying "Don't say that, because you are somebody." As you probably noticed, her words always stuck.

So during a phase were I became a Muslim and dedicated my journey of life to the beliefs and ways of Islam, I took up learning Arabic and became pretty good at reading, reciting, and understanding certain surahs (scriptures) in the Quran. I even learned how to write different expressions that I wanted to with little to no problem. Upon further seeking and gaining knowledge of the different words of the Aramaic language, I stumbled across one that was all too familiar. I've said this word plenty of times as a child growing up, and I even heard it quite often on the cartoons I used to watch. The word it seemed would always be used as a saying to make magic appear. Honestly, I've always thought it was some made up word that different magicians used for their magic tricks. For that reason, it never occurred to me to actually define the word itself for my own understanding. However this day when there was nothing better to do I researched it. What I found out changed my outlook on words for rest of my life and right here in this 16th chapter of *Be The Greatest You* I'm going to share it. I only warn you first to strap up your boots and take seat because this may knock you off your feet. What I had learned was that "abracadabra" is actually a word and it means, "What I speak is what I create." I found that very interesting, and I tell you when I read that I was lifted—I mean downright astonished. I don't know how many times I repeated that to myself, over and over again. Once I learned that what I speak is what I create, I most certainly used that newfound knowledge to my own benefit. I redirected my whole outlook on words and stopped calling myself so many things I once did. I also changed and directed the words I used and how I used them.

Words can do any and everything, from sparking up a movement to inspiring you to rise up above adversity. Words are one of your most creative sources of creating power. Words can get you the love of your life and connect your hearts. On the other hand, words can take you down a dark path with self-doubt and destroy your creativity, as well as your relationships. You should know how powerful words are and, yet, it's scary how little attention we pay to our words. You may or may not realize how powerful your words truly are in terms of influencing the results you're getting in your life. You should challenge yourself to use your words more consciously so that you can move toward what you want to create. Utilize the power in words so that you can become more collaborative, more innovative, and more creative. It would help you to look at life's obstacles in different ways so that you can transform your life, your relationships, your team, or your workplace.

I want you to think about your words in two ways—creative or limited. Are your words creative? Are they uplifting? Are they inspiring? Are they proactive? Or are they negative? Are they destructive? Are they humiliating? Just understand that the difference between creative and limiting can be a really powerful tool for you. It may sound real minute, extremely small, but just being conscious of your words can make a huge difference in your life. Ask yourself, are your words that you're using right now moving you toward what you want? Or are they moving you toward what you don't want? Just by being conscious, you can have an abracadabra mentality knowing that what you speak is what you create, and start using words that are moving you toward what you want and what you want to create. Let's look at abracadabra on three levels: (1) a personal level, (2) an interpersonal level, and (3) from a leadership perspective.

First the personal level. Despite what some may say, we all talk to ourselves, and you're not crazy for doing so. You have this constant stream of thoughts going on. In these thoughts you have carefully designed words that influence what you believe and what you see. The internal thoughts that we all have going on are similar. They're there to influence what you believe and what you see and, consequently, what you end up creating in life. Skills and knowledge are required, but oftentimes they're not sufficient. More often than not it's the inner thoughts that get in the way. You can still possess the skills and the knowledge, but sometimes the thoughts you have still get in the way and what you speak is what you create.

On an interpersonal level, by saying what I speak is what I create is something you may have been blind to. But through this reading you may have now become aware of it, and that's exactly what everyone needs in order to teach some people. Think about it, if you had that kind of relationship with people you're around most, you could help each other overcome these self-limiting words and thoughts you tend to use. You would then build up a team of pillars, a support base that would then help you snap out of it when you're discouraged, or motivate you when you're fighting fatigue.

On a leadership level, words are a bit more critical, because leaders (well, a great leader anyway) in my experience creates hope. One of the ways they do so, is to tell an inspiring story about where the business or team is going while they enable people to understand their role in the story, where they fit in, and how their contribution is helping create this amazing future. If you're a leader and your people don't understand and aren't inspired by where you're going and they don't see their place in it, then you're not leading.

A few steps in putting the word abracadabra "what I speak is what I create" to use, is first to simply start by being aware. Are the words you're using creative or limiting? Be aware! Second, monitor your internal language, as well as your external language. Use the term as a quick tool to notice when you're not using words that are moving toward the future you want to create or complimenting your goals. Fourth, when you see results that aren't the results you want, do a little reflecting, do a little examination under the surface and consider whether or not the words that you're thinking throughout your mental capacity are getting in your way. Lastly, you can journal about what it is that you're trying to create. Write about what the future looks like for you in vivid description and detail. Write about it until picturing the thoughts about it make you smile. By choosing your words carefully, the words you use with yourself and others can move toward hope, and just know, "what you speak is what you create."

Words themselves symbolize the power of speech. The power of speech evokes an emotion and a response. It instills in people the need to respond with whatever you're presenting them with. The letters of our so-called sacred alphabet also have incredible hidden powers. Therefore when you learn to decipher words and use them wisely, you can command the forces of the universe to manifest a world of love, abundance, and prosperity. Certain words in their own right refer to cosmic intelligence. It's similar to how we assign a sound to each letter of the alphabet and use the alphabet to speak words of different sounds and vibrations. The words that describe our feelings, emotions, and moods are intelligent energy. These words help us to communicate with each other and carry the power to contain intelligence.

For instance, you're driving your car and suddenly there's an issue, most people decide to control the issue and listen to the words in their minds that assure them they can fix the problem. Why do the words that we encounter have such a wide range of effects on us? Because many of the brain regions that process language also control the inside of your body, including major organs and systems. These brain regions guide your heart beat and adjust the glucose entering your bloodstream to fuel your cells. So words are tools for regulating human bodies. Other people's words directly affect your brain activity and your bodily systems, and your words have the same effect on other people. Whether you intend that effect or not is irrelevant, it's just how we're wired.

Throughout your life you have developed a habit of self-conversations that create your beliefs. Some beliefs you acquire are positive and others negative. The negative thoughts prevent you from reaching your goals, like "I'm terrible at interviews," "I'm nothing like the other candidates, it's no way they're going to hire me." But the best part here is that you can always change these negative beliefs into positive beliefs. You can say, "I have all the necessary skills and experience, I'm the perfect candidate for this position."

Affirmations are positive statements that send positive messages to your brain and reprogram your conscious mind. If

179

you ever had someone tell you that you couldn't do something or made you feel that you weren't enough, you can be sure that those messages are hidden in your subconscious mind ready to derail you at any time. Positive comments, such as "You're doing great," "I'm the best at what I do," coming up with great ideas or completing a task will help you feel satisfied and work harder. You must always try to take criticism positively, and remind yourself that no matter how challenging a task is, you can do it. Believe in yourself. Using "I am" affirmation encourages you to bring positive changes to your life: "I am strong, I am worthy, I have what it takes, I can do it, I can make it happen" are powerful messages that can help you transform yourself the way you want and change your life. "I am" affirmations help you to avoid those negative thoughts and fill your mind with gratitude, abundance, and joy. Affirmations are a self-help strategy that promotes self-confidence and belief in your abilities.

You've probably affirmed yourself without even realizing it by telling yourself things like, "I'm successful; I'm confident; I'm powerful; I am getting better and better every day; All I need is within me right now; I am an unstoppable force of nature; I'm living with abundance; and I'm having a positive and inspiring impact on the people I'm coming in contact with or through my work." Using these statements regularly can shift the focus from your failures toward your strengths. Repeating these affirmations can help boost your motivation and confidence, but you still have to take some actions yourself. Think of affirmations as a step toward change, not the change itself.

What can be spoken can become your reality. A thought or an idea that can be formed into a word can become real. It usually works like this: what you think is what you speak, and what you speak becomes your reality. So when you hear your parents or people say things like, "You are useless, You're nothing, You can't do anything right, You are ugly, What a waste, or Nothing good will ever come to you," and if you believe them, they can become your reality. More and more today I see the power of words affecting our young people, and some of the behaviors we see are despicable and downright disgusting. We as people, and especially the youth who are our future leaders are believing many of the lies that they are hearing about themselves, so they carry out actions in our inner cities, behaving the way negative, judgmental people expect them to behave.

These toxic negative words are becoming their reality, even to the point of harming someone and harming themselves. It's easy enough to understand that this is a world of good and evil, but words are used like weapons of mass destruction rather than fueling hope and encouragement. It's time we stop ignoring the power of words and give them the respect they deserve. You may have heard that you're worthless, useless, ugly, fat, stupid, hated, and just a waste of time. Well I encourage you to believe the opposite. Start by telling yourself that you're beautiful inside and out, that you're smart and intelligent. Tell yourself that you are loved, and you are not only worthy but worthy of being loved.

The power of words is color blind. The power of words has no respect of what social status you fall under. The power of words doesn't care about your ambition, or plans for the future. The power of words can make you or break you. You and you alone are the filter that determines what words have the power over your heart, your mind, and your life. You and you alone are responsible for allowing the words to become the reality of your life. When you come to a point in embracing the reality that there is power in words and the understanding of how words can indeed hurt you, give them the respect they deserve and you'll start to see change in your own life as miracles and blessings come forth. When you do that you'll start to see those same changes and miracles in others as well. "Trust me!"

CHAPTER 17

The Importance of Education

*"Education is the key to unlocking the world.
It is the passport to freedom."*
—Oprah Winfrey

"What I don't know won't hurt me." When I was growing up I used to hear this quite often, and I'll even be honest to say that at one point in time I used to believe this saying. That is until I got a little older, put some thought into it and came to realize that it has to be the most stupid, backwards, anti-intelligent phrase that was ever created. In fact, because of what you don't know may be the reason why a lot of what you may have endured, for example, hard times in life that you had to overcome and financial situations you may have experienced, could have, would have, and should have been avoided. Primarily what you don't know is exactly why you are or aren't where you want to be in life right now. Now that I'm all grown up and see life for what it is and how it really works, I fully support the phrase, "If I knew better, I'd do better." In this chapter we're going to explore the concept of an education, the importance of an adequate education, the contribution to the hindrances caused by the foundational public educational system, and uselessness of its utilization in the real world. Let's began, shall we?

Let me ask you, when you think of education, what's the first thought that comes to your mind? Is it the educational system, schools, universities, or possibly graduating and receiving your degree or a certificate? Or perhaps you haven't taken the time to contemplate on this much yet. The importance of education is far beyond any simplistic explanation. It's for this reason that we're going to take a real look at the purpose of education. Prepare yourself, some of this information (depending on where you're at in life) is going to benefit you for the rest of your life.

What is the purpose of an education and the meaning of being educated? The purpose of an education is to unleash your own unique limitless potential, and to learn how to make it meaningful and valuable for/in society. Education will enable you to adjust and learn how to shape the future. This goes beyond being prepared for the future, because it's very difficult to prepare for something that's continuously changing. It's more based on being able to be in charge of your future and with it the future of the world and those people and relatives who come after you. The purpose of education and being educated is so you can understand and master the conditions for continual development. We are all living on the same planet and whether we realize it or not, we are all dealing with each other's problems and fighting each other's wars. We breathe the same air and we acquire the same natural resources. We can try to set borders and build walls but at the end of the day, we have to learn how to deal with one another and live among each other. Through being educated you learn how to master much-needed qualities to be successful, such as empathy, respect for others, and outer cultural awareness, just to name a few. Being educated shows you how to live a happy and healthy lifestyle.

Education is one of the many blessings in life, as well as one of its necessities. It's the most empowering force of the world. It creates knowledge, boosts confidence, and breaks down the barriers of opportunity. It's a subject that has been studied for thousands of years and has played a role in many areas of human life. From ancient civilization to modern times, education has been used to solve problems, make predictions, and understand

184

the world around us. "Education is our passport to the future, for tomorrow belongs only to the people who prepare for it today." That's a quote from the honorable late, great Malcolm X, who became known as "Malcolm el-Hajj Malik el-Shabazz," which roughly translates to "The Pilgrim Malcolm the Patriarch." I agree with that passage to this day.

This is because education is the cloth of our society; it's the fabric of our civilization that binds us together, that helps us understand one another, and that helps us understand the world. It plays a very important role in everyone's life. It is very necessary to live a great and better life therefore it's very important to get a proper education. You see, a good education will always increase your confidence level, shape you, and remove all the doubts while adapting to all the changes and challenges in your life. It's the tool that can keep you happy and peaceful, as well as make you a better socialized human being.

Education encompasses you and your surroundings, and affects your insights, decisions, and influences. I think it's really important to gain insight into who you are as a person and what makes you unique. Your unique skills, what you love doing, what you're good at, what drives you, and who you naturally are. But not much as in this is who I am in stagnated sense but, rather, how can I improve myself, how can I grow as a human being? On the insight side of it as to have an "Oh I get it," "It all makes sense now," or "Now I understand it" moment. On the influence side, to be able to make things better, to improve your life, and to have an impact on the world. To push the boundaries of what is and what isn't known to us as of right now.

Now you probably heard while you were growing up to do well, study hard in school, and get good grades because that would help you get into college or get a good job and, in return, you'll have a successful life. Your parents may assume that a good education would make you happy, so in their case education was necessary, only because in their minds it would help provide you with the life they feel you want. This is how most families, parents, and individuals think. They value education because they understand it's important. But what is education really, and what is its purpose? What is this thing that people value so much? Is education a tool that helps you get a good job after you graduate? Or just accumulated debt that drags you down for years after? Well, maybe we should dig a little deeper.

You see most of our parents and maybe even you, perhaps, thought that education means to get good grades and have great manners. However, and let me apologize first if this happens to burst your bubble, but a real education is beyond just earning degrees, and it goes beyond any systematic instruction. The real purpose of education is to elevate your consciousness. The real purpose of education is to evolve yourself. Education is meant to help reach a higher state of being. Assuming that education is important because it can help you get a good job after you graduate is dangerous. If you see things that way you're just limiting yourself, and by receiving student loans you put yourself in debt for that.

Education is crucial, because it's the only way you can develop a holistic understanding of the world and, yes, that would no doubt make you much happier. As a human being there are different stages and phases you need to go through in life. Abraham Maslow was a famous psychologist who developed a theory of psychological health based on human needs and priorities. This theory has often been referred to as Maslow's hierarchy of needs. Now according to his theory there are six tiers in the pyramid, all of which contain different sets of human needs.

186

The first tier is called physiological needs, and it refers to the basic needs we all need to stay alive, such as air, water, food, sleep, and so forth. This tier is pretty apparent as you cannot live without meeting these needs. The second tier is safety needs and, once you've fulfilled your physiological needs, your safety needs must be met. This tier includes thing like a house, resources, such as employment, and being able to secure your property. Once you've got those needs satisfied there is a set of needs called love and belongingness. As you might assume this includes needs like having honorable friends, trustworthy relationships with your spouse, friends and family, and passionate intimacy with your significant other. The fourth tier is self-esteem. In this tier the needs are fulfilled in having recognition, importance, confidence, and respect from others. Only after those needs are relatively satisfied, that you get into the tender tier part of life, and this tier is called self-actualization. It's here where you can feel the need to be more creative, to develop a higher sense of morality, to be more spontaneous, to solve problems, to make discoveries, accept facts and feel the need to contribute more to society. The last tier, self-transcendence, is all about true spirituality and enlightenment. In this tier you feel the need to become more aware. You want to develop unconditional love and attain new levels of consciousness.

The real purpose of education is to help your get through all these phases and stages, so that you can meet your needs. Education should be the vehicle to get you to the top of this ladder of needs. Don't make the mistake that many others make; do not assume that your education will stop one day or that you'll be subjected to and stuck between those lower tiers and become unhappy like many others. Education isn't a destination, it's a journey. A lot of people stop seeking education after graduation, because they assume it's enough to live a rich and healthy life. Clearly, what they were missing was the real purpose and meaning of education. Education is a never-ending process, you must work on educating and developing yourself up until the moment you die.

Where does this misconception come from? Why do most people believe that education is only important because it could help them get a good job and that education should stop after graduation? Now I'm not saying that what you may think or what you were told is wrong. I'm just saying it's partially correct. Going to school, having good manners, and being well behaved is part of your education by today's social standards. What most people support about education is due to what was strictly shaped by the culture in which they live. For example, some people from different countries do not even consider things like manners as part of their education. Think of those who live in tribes, they don't care about their manners. The only thing they care about is their survival. Therefore their education revolves around being able to hunt, cook, and build shelters as they have different needs. What I'm aiming at by even using this analogy is the fact that education is strictly defined by factors, such as your culture, education system, family, friends, and the environment you live in.

The value of continuing and the furthering your education is insight. When you continue to seek knowledge, you get this insight into the world and how you can maneuver through it while benefiting your wants and desires. Different aspects and experiences in life, such as the corporate world as we know it compared to the underworld as it's usually described, are good because you get different insights about how the world in general works. With expanding your education comes intuition,

188

creativity, leadership, identity, entrepreneurship, critical thinking, imagination, and inventiveness. It's those who not only seek a higher education but apply their intelligence to their natural creativity who has contributed to the innovative world that we live in today. That's what you should be striving for, not to be like anyone else but to challenge yourself intellectually to potentially stamp your mark in the natural progression within our society to this ever-evolving civilization.

CHAPTER 18

Knowledge of Being Creative & Being Versatile

"Creativity is seeing what others see
and thinking what no one else ever thought."
—Albert Einstein

There's an almost mystical, spiritual sensation you feel when being focused and exercising your creative abilities. A lot of people are missing out on this feeling, and I feel there are too many who are not even in tune with the smallest percent of their potential. I think honestly that this is a great insult to your God-given talents. It's a shame how an enormous number of people end up taking their own lives, stuck in depression, or just wasting their entire life simply because they fail to realize or actualize their untapped potential and creativity.

We seem to be in an era in which we're not really teaching our children how to be creative, and if they do become creative it's through their own curiously self-taught efforts. We don't have a careful or diligent process for teaching people how to be creative, how to find their creative calling, what they want to be creative in, and all the different ways creativity can manifest itself. Often when you mention creativity people automatically think of art or music, and that they're not an artist or a musician, therefore they can't be creative. But there are so many different ways to be creative—you can be creative in business, social media, day-to-day activities, communicating with other people, even in your relationships and your expressions of romance.

Everyone can be creative, believe it or not. A lot of people tend to think that creativity is paired—either you have it or you don't—but in reality we do all have it. It's just a matter of how you interpret it. You may think, "Well, I'm not an artist so I don't use creativity at work." But it's more than just an artistic expression. Whether you're working in retail, an office job, or even if you're a professional athlete, you're probably using creativity to make decisions or solve problems on the day-to-day basis.

Creativity is both a skill and a process. It's something you can learn and, like any other skill, it's something that you can get better at if you practice and repeatedly use it. Now you might think, "Well I don't have time to sit down and create something every day." This is where it's important to realize the difference between using creativity and actually creating something. You know in a lot of ways creativity is all about how you see things so, yeah, you can use it to create poems or paintings but you can also use it in practical ways like coming up with an alternate solution for a work project, or organizing things in your home. So the next time you think, "I'm not creative," or "I'm not as creative as some of the other people," take a step back and really take look at what it is you do on the daily basis. You might be surprised at how often you're using your creativity.

Being creative and utilizing your creativity is not just a way you can earn money or find something to do while finding yourself being bored. You have to see it for something much deeper. It may actually be your way of connecting to consciousness. Your creativity can be a way of honoring and appreciating your collective abilities. When you really appreciate creativity, it's not enough just to envision and dream about it—you want to participate in it. You find yourself wanting to participate in your overall creative ideas.

Being creative also fosters change. Thinking creatively helps you to think about new possibilities and can help us turn

191

the ordinary into the extraordinary. In fact, being creative has been compared to meditation for its calming effects on the mind as well as the body. A creative act, such as gardening or sewing actually releases dopamine, our brain's natural antidepressant. Being creative helps to reduce anxiety, depression, or stress, and it even helps you process trauma. In fact, studies have shown that painting or drawing helps people express trauma or experiences that they find difficult to put into words, and writing or keeping a journal helps you manage emotions in a much more productive way. Playing musical instruments has been found to improve left and right brain hemispheric connectivity.

So, as you can see, there are many benefits of being creative, and here are more you may not have thought about. Being creative helps promote self-discoveries. It helps you understand what you like and what you don't like. Being creative helps you promote planning and problem-solving as well as thinking, thereby improving general cognition. It also puts you into your happy zone and, because creativity is a form of play, it improves a sense of well-being from your accomplishments. Because creativity requires commitment and dedication it also strengthens essential life skills, such as focus and discipline. Creativity also encourages us to become lifelong learners. So a challenge to you is what are you going to do today and every day during your time of leisure—to do something differently, to do something creatively.

The more you start to appreciate your life as this creative consciousness, this work of art, you start to see the miracle of your life. As you get in touch with the magic of it, you then want to devote and dedicate your life on its behalf. That's when you start to connect to life, that's when your life becomes meaningful. When you start to live your life through your creativity, that's when each and every single day becomes precious. It becomes sensational, because you then start to live in the spiritual meaning of your purpose in life.

I want you to consider this encouragement I'm giving you right here, versus the typical attitude you may have toward your life. The typical attitude in which you wake up and you're just running around doing the rat race stuff you're used to doing, like going to work, running errands, paying your bills, doing what your boss told you to do. It's living how someone you don't even know tells you how to live in order to accumulate the "American dream" and retire late in your life when there's little to no life left in you to enjoy. Notice how different these attitudes are, the disconnect from beauty, the wonders of the world, the miraculous nature of life through your creativeness from a typical programmed lifestyle most people are accustomed to live, yet have the nerve to complain about.

Yeah that's why they become disillusioned about life, and that's how they become depressed. Because, honestly, what joy can there be? How can you love life living that way? Even more so at that point, your life doesn't belong to you and life itself has more control of you than you have control of it. Taking into consideration that you only have this one life to live, don't be that person. Because then you're living your life jumping through practical hoops trying to minimize your suffering and pain. Trying your best not to get yelled at by your boss, or scrutinized for not showing up or finishing your work on time is not a positive, constructive way to live. It's just living life along the path of least resistance. It's like a situation in which you're just going to school and doing your homework so your parents don't yell at you sort of thing. Or you're just doing the bare minimum so you don't get fired or lose your job, so you can continue to pay your bills, watch Netflix, stay entertained by following or watching someone else's lifestyle just to do it all over again tomorrow. Don't keep on letting life live you, when you should be living life.

If you're going to live a life outside of your creative ingenuity, you might as well not even live at all. You're wasting your life and, deep down, your soul and your spirit. You feel it, you know it, you know you're living below your full potential, and if you ask how I know, it's because I was there. You should be unsatisfied with that sort of lifestyle. That's a signal your spirit is sending to you that you have to be able to decode, and knowing you're not living life in alignment with your highest values. When you're in that mindset, you start to think "Yeah, what is the meaning of all this? Why was I even born? What's the purpose of life? Why is God so cruel? Why would he even make me like this and put me here?" or "Why would he even create something like this?"

The amazing thing about life is that you get to construct it the way you want it to be. You are in complete charge of your role in the movie of life. You're the actor, screenwriter, producer, editor, and that's what makes life so amazing. If you don't construct your creative consciousness, then it's like you're not even living at all, and it can't be wonderful. But if you take conscious control and you realize you're in a big playground, you can build whatever you want. It really doesn't matter what you build. You may think, "Well why should I build or create anything when eventually I'm going to die?" Then I would have to agree; however, you have others, possibly children, with their lives ahead of them that you can lend a head start to in life. But overall it doesn't matter what you built or what you created, it's solely about how you spent your life living while gifted with this one chance to live it. Are you going to live with limited intentions, or are you going to live with purpose and make something out of your life? That's really what life is affording you through living out of your creativity.

Now I purposely separated discussing the ability of being versatile with the chapter where I discussed the importance of being able to adjust. Although they may appear hand in hand, if it were my choice for inspiring you to be the greatest you then I would encourage you to be more versatile in your creativeness than your adaptability. In any environment or any settings, once you adjust or adapt then you automatically inherited the ability to become versatile. Once you apply being versatile with your creativeness, then you're building up a different monster—a whole greater force, one to be reckoned with.

You may have heard about the *Sun and Wind* wager to see who can get the man's coat off. So the wind goes first and blows extremely hard, and the man just grips his coat tighter around him, hunches his shoulders, and pushes himself to move forward. The sun then takes a turn and just shines brightly on the man. Then feeling unbearably hot, he proceeds to casually take off his coat, sits down, and takes in the view. So the lesson we need to consider here is that by gripping tightly and forcing a situation to be a certain specific way, you may actually be making things worse. Whereas, if you were more relaxed, open, and creatively versatile about the situation, you may very well end up with a much healthier and harmonious result.

So being versatile means to have a wide variety of skills. The term "Jack of all trades" refers to a person who is knowledgeable in many different skills or areas of life. It usually refers to a person who is versatile, and who can adapt to many different situations and tasks. If someone or something is versatile, it can be used in many different situations or used for many different things. So being versatile could only make you more resourceful and able to handle a variety of situations should life present them to you.

The law of versatility is an important principle to understand, one that applies in your personal and professional life. Being versatile could bring you many benefits, but it needs to be the right balance of versatility along with creativity that achieves success. Your natural ability to be versatile can be your greatest asset. The law of versatility is an ideal of having multiple skills, strengths, experiences, and talents that give you an advantage over those who solely focus on one field. Being creative gives you the ability to not only top the bar, but you tend to recreate the bar. This will cover all areas of your life whether it's in your career, relationships, hobbies, or goals and various pursuits in life. By embracing the laws of a versatile creativity, you can grow a variety of capabilities and be better prepared for what life throws your way. A benefit of applying your versatile creativity is having multiple skill sets and mindsets at your disposal. This would allow you to adapt to different circumstances and improve them when needed, making you an important asset to the situation at hand. For example, if you have experiences in different industries, such as marketing and finances you'll be able to leverage you're knowledge in both fields by potentially starting your own company.

The same would go for your personal development. You can develop multiple interests that could create growth in many aspects of your life. Possessing the ability of being versatile can make you a well-rounded person, who could handle any situation with finesse and grace. Adding your creativity can allow you to navigate through these difficult scenarios, displaying an edge over those who only know one way to approach a problem. This makes it easier to make appropriate decisions for what's best for yourself as well as those around you. It's important to know that creative versatility gives you the ability to take risks without fear, because you'll know that there's always something else to fall back on in a case things don't go as planned.

Becoming creatively versatile starts with analyzing yourself and understanding what skill set would be beneficial for you, your goals, and your dreams. One way to do this is by talking to those who have experienced success in similar fields, so that you can learn from their experiences and get ideas for what paths can best work for you moving forward. Reading books with related topics that interest you is another great way to extract that creative versatile side of you without needing direct guidance from someone else. Overall embracing the law of versatility, incorporated with your God-given creativity is essential if you want to stay ahead of this ever-changing world while achieving personal growth along the way. By developing multiple skill sets, mindsets, interest, and talents you would be able to open up more opportunities for yourself while gaining valuable experiences that will help you grow both professionally and personally throughout your life.

CHAPTER 19

The Knowledge of Being a Good Follower to Become a Great Leader

"He who could not be a great follower
cannot be a great leader."
—Aristotle

Are you a good follower? Do your leaders appreciate you for being a good follower? We tend to pay a lot of attention to leadership, but in this chapter I'm going to base my message on followership, the importance of being a good follower, to think about what followership is, the impact that great followership can have, and why the world needs great followers. Now I don't want my message to get misconstrued, so let me first put down the point I aim for you to pick up so as not to be misquoted by the message I'm trying to convey. I know some of us can be a little headstrong as to admit, claim, or live by the means of being a follower. I can be guilty of this because I like to consider myself a natural born leader, so I can relate and because of that I felt more of a need to state this little disclaimer. But as I get into this topic I only ask that you think outside the box and, like the great Andre "Gorgeous Dre" Taylor would say, "Bring your whole mind." Now if you are an employee and currently work under an employer, you are being led. If you have a supervisor, manager, tutor, mentor, agent, foreman, journeyman, deacon, big homie, O.G., or a boss you are being led. And to go deeper into the point I'm trying to make, if you are being led, that makes you a follower. So with that being said let's get into being a good follower to become a greater leader.

There is a saying that goes, "If you think you are leading and you turn around and look behind you and no one is following you, then you're just going for a walk." Followers are more important to leaders than leaders are to followers. A follower shares in an influential relationship among leaders and other followers with intent to support leaders who share their mutual purpose. If you search the internet, there's no lack of resources for inspiring to be good and effective leaders. Many would tell you if you want to make sure you are a great leader then make sure you are seen as a leader and not a follower. Even if you don't feel like it, just fake it until you make it. In my opinion that has to be some of worst advice ever given. That's like the blind faking to have vision leading the fellow blind until they make it. That would be insanely crazy, right? This would mean you should seek out opportunities to take charge, adopt, and associate with people who are seen as leaders. Show confidence, take on a power role, and make sure you show superiority over your peers. I really doubt that anyone would become a leader by doing this, based on the fact that this person would lack the experience.

What does it mean to be a great follower? Great followers find others doing great things and put their time and energy into helping others succeed. Let's discuss ways to become a better follower, knowing that becoming a better follower will make you better leader. You'll hear me say, "The best leaders come from being great followers," and I'm convinced that this is true because most leaders have spent a lot of time following before they assume their position of leadership. A varsity football player spent around three years playing with the team before he was eligible to be the team captain. An Army Rangers platoon sergeant spends years on a fire team perfecting his skills as an infantryman before he's given a leadership position. The junior assistant was a valued member of the business for several years before she became the project manager. An electrician spent at least five years as an apprentice before qualifying him/her to become a journeyman in even making him/her eligible to become a foreman. In all of these situations the leaders developed their skills as a follower before assuming their role as a leader. Let's take a look at what's considered to be the most important characteristics of great followership, such as obedience, competence, being pro-active, asking for help, volunteering, asking the uncomfortable questions, and knowing how to follow.

There's a misconception to being a leader and being a follower. All leaders need to follow something so that they can lead, and every follower learns how to lead by following. The problem is nobody wants to be or considered to be a follower anymore. It amazes me how we all collect followers through our social media pages, but no one wants to fit in the category of being a follower. I think that's because we always see following as something weak or something submissive, especially when we hear things like, "Real leaders don't follow." As a student of life, I would like to say that I'm a proud lifetime follower. I follow those people who may have come before me or those who have found success in like-minded ideals. I follow my dreams and the directions of my short-term goals to make the long-term accomplishments achievable. So being a follower isn't weak at all, it's a highly skilled process of collaborations and cooperation. It's also doing something either beside or behind someone that would otherwise be more difficult or impossible to learn.

Followers help facilitate the process of completion, they also help something or someone become successful. They assist in moving things along. If there weren't any followers, the leader would have trouble getting things done not to mention doing things on their own. One cannot create a movement by themselves. You need great followers in order to accomplish that. Any great leader would admit that if not for an even greater follower his accomplishments would be that much more unattainable, if not impossible.

You can't be a good follower if you can't do what you're told. If you are a follower of a certain leader, team, or group you must be obedient to the best interest of the group. You don't just become a leader because you want to be a leader. A great leader has to have experience about a lot of things. This knowledge would be in experience from A to Z—from the bottom to the top—and the only way leaders would have had these experiences is if they were once a follower of some kind to learn to do, to understand, and to equip themselves with the knowledge of how to operate things under an umbrella of a group, team, business, or any type of entity. We've seen throughout history a lot of leaders fail because they have never been a dedicated follower, or just plain failed at being a follower yet somehow found themselves in a position of leadership that wasn't earned or deserved. They never started from a base point or the bottom, so without that understanding it's naturally hard for them or anyone who wants to be a leader to understand their subordinates. If you want to be a great leader, it's imperative that you become a great follower. Any leaders who were successful in their lifetime in this universe were usually the people who were great followers at some point of time in their life.

One of the most basic qualifications of leadership is great humility. As I read up and researched the attributes of all these great leaders, what I found interesting is that although the leaders may be the motivators, they may be the visionaries and the great designers of change, it was the followers who got things done, and it was the followers who made things happen. If you have something to follow, something that's bigger than you are, something that gives you a sense of identity, a sense of purpose, a sense of value, then that does two things: The first is helping to prevent that state of depression that many people have experienced these days; the second is, if you have felt yourself subject to the state of depression it helps you on your road to recovery. The job of a great follower is to set and create the conditions for the leader to do a wonderful job. If leadership is the spark, then followership is the flame. I believe that you can do every bit as much of what you want in this world right now by being a great follower as you can by being a great leader. But I further believe that it will be the great followers of today who will prosper to be the great leaders of tomorrow.

In reality there would never be any real effective leaders unless there were faithful followers. The truth is leaders are only as effective as their ability to engage followers, because without followership, leadership is nothing, it's next to non-existent. Exceptionally gifted leaders are rare. Most leaders start at the bottom, they take entry-level positions, and work their way up earning their position. They learn about what motivates their co-workers, they learn about teamwork, and how to work well together to achieve goals. They develop empathy and compassion for people they work with. They learn this from becoming good followers who are passionately committed, deeply involved, and actively supporting their great leaders. In reality, they are learning key followership traits that will assist them well when they eventually become leaders themselves.

So the question would then become, "How do I lead others?" Knowing how to lead others is important, but in today's world it's more important that people give you the permission to lead them. When people understand how you're going to develop them, they will agree to how and where you're leading them. It's not that you lead by power in this time and era we are living in, it's more that you lead by convincing. With that, understand that you have to have much more flexibility in your mentality and in your life.

A major challenge in being a great leader is to recognize that followers differ substantially in talent and motivation. Similarly, a challenge in becoming an effective follower is to understand your basic value to being a group member. So let's look at the type of followers.

There are ways to classify how followers differ from one another. At one end of the scale is the feeling and doing of nothing. At the other end is being passionately committed and deeply involved. Isolated followers are completely detached and passively support how things stand by not taking actions to bring about change. They don't care much about their leaders and just do their job without taking an interest in the overall organization. They usually need coaching, and getting rid of them is typically the best or only solution. Bystanders are freeloaders who typically simply detach when it fits their self-interest. These are the ones who, during meetings have to continuously step out or are constantly checking their phones for missed calls and text messages. They usually have low motivation, so the leader has to work extra hard to find the right motivators to spark the bystander into action. Now the participants will show enough engagement to invest some of their own time and money to make a difference, such as taking the initiative to learn new ways to help the leader or the group. The participants are sometimes for and sometimes against the leader and the business at hand. The leader may have to observe their work and attitudes to make sure they are being constructive as well as productive. However, participants have also been looked at as active followers or those who make major contributions to the overall mission. Activists are engaged and heavily invested in people and processes, and they're eager to show their support. They feel strongly, whether it be positive or negatively about their leader and the organization. Then you have the diehard types who are super engaged, so much to point that they are willing to go down for their own cause, or willing to off the leader if they feel they're being led in the wrong direction. The diehards can be an asset or a liability to the leader, group, or cause. Diehards can have an even stronger tendency to be whistle-blowers than the activist. Leaders have to stay in touch with diehards to see if their energy is being pointed in the interest of the organization. The category of followers highlights the challenging role of leaders. Not everybody in the group is eager to collaborate toward obtaining organizational goals.

A great quote from author Miles Monroe states, "Every human has the instinct and capacity for leadership, but most do not have the courage or will to cultivate it." Meaning we all have it in us to do so, but not everyone is willing to take the necessary steps. It's because leadership is in us all. All of the greatest leaders, of every era and every generation rose to an occasion that something deeply rooted inside of them either realized that this is wrong, I have to make a difference, I have to take a stand, or maybe someone else said, "I believe in you, and I will follow you," and therefore that person became a leader. I find that the best leaders tend to be the best followers. The reason they achieve rank is because they saw themselves in service of something greater than themselves. Whether it was a cause or whether it was a vision, they saw themselves of service. In other words, they saw themselves in the state of following. It's this thought in action that has gained them the trust of those below and above them.

CHAPTER 20

The Knowledge of Reacting vs. Responding

"Life is 10% about what happens to you and 90% how you react to it."
—Charles R. Swindoll

Do you usually find yourself in overwhelming situations, or getting into things that you stop and wonder or ask yourself questions like, "How the hell did I get myself into this?" "What did I do to deserve this?" or "Why is this happening to me?" Again, in my life I have asked myself these very same questions, and I'm sure others have as well so don't feel alone. When I did stop to think about it, I had to go to the root of the circumstance and see how it all grew to become the problem or how it landed me in undesirable situations time and time again. The seeds that grew into a tree of my current problems have always been me, my own doings, and my ways of thinking. Whether it was the course of actions I willed myself to take, words I decided to use, decisions that I made, it all stemmed from me and how I chose to react to the circumstance. Now that I think about it, ever since I was younger getting in all sorts of trouble, my mom would say, "Son, you don't think, you react." At the time I didn't know what she meant, because truthfully all I did was think. Some people have even told me that I think too much. What I didn't grasp at that time was the fact that I was reacting instead of responding, and that there was a big difference between the two.

In this chapter I'm going to tackle the difference between reacting and responding, and the effect one can have over the other. I'm going to address the two, the difference they make on whether you do or don't have what you want in life, and how they play on whether you are or aren't where you want to be within your current position in life. Remember, change doesn't just come, and sometimes it's up to you to make change an option by creating opportunity when it doesn't present itself. You may not recognize it, but the universe presents matters to create change within your life constantly, daily, consistently through every second of every moment you're awake. That's just the 10% of it, the 90% are the decisions you make because of it.

Let's look at the difference in the words for their natural meaning, shall we? Now reaction or reacting is immediate. It's a habit-based way of interacting, which is why it can be very patterned. For example, things will happen in the world, you'll feel some kind of way, and you'll do some kind of thing. The more you observe yourself in those moments, the more you'll see how set on autopilot you are. This means no matter how much it happens outside of your awareness, it's like your actions are programmed into you. It's thinking unconsciously, whereas responding is more of an objectively conscious way of thinking or interacting in the present moment. So reacting is pretty much embedded in you through your accustomed ways of handling a particular situation, but responding is when you have a choice and how you choose to handle the situation, so to speak.

The reason I felt the need to differentiate the two is because so many of us are so used to living in that autopilot reactive state of mind, and you can feel so ashamed or disappointed in your reactions at times. I know I have, and sometimes still do. Say, for an example, you hear someone say something or you receive a text that makes you feel angry. Typically what do you do when you're angry? You do one of a few things, you either lash out, shut down, or just disassociate with that person. So let's say you lash out and then the matter escalates because the person you lashed out at has something to say in return, and now you're finding yourself in a conflict. Well, if you're like many of us in a time of conflict, you can say or do things from an emotional place that you don't necessarily mean. What happens after the fact for many people is the feeling of being ashamed or disappointed. Afterwards you can usually find yourself feeling like you stooped to a lower level, acted smaller than you are by conducting yourself in this out-of-control way, and possibly not even agreeing with everything you said or did based on an emotional reaction. This is the difficult part, because this is that autopilot state of mind I spoke about taking over at the time when you aren't even in control of yourself and making all of the decisions for you.

Life is like a movie that you star in as the main character, and everything you do is considered to be an act. Either you do it consciously or you do it compulsively. But when you do it compulsively you think that it's real, when actually it's an act. Because all thoughts start off in your brain, everything with regard to this act has already been cooked up in your mind. So if these thoughts are in your head, do you want to generate them consciously or compulsively? That's all making a choice is. But making choices on compulsive thinking is a self-destructive way to live. If everything that's done is done as an act because you're reacting from a memory, an experience, or an influence, at least do it consciously, that way life becomes beautiful and not a trap of misery. When you make compulsive decisions, it starts to look like life is against you, God is punishing you, or you're experiencing bad luck in living life with a dark cloud over you. The only way to look at your situation like it's a trap is if a way out of it never presents itself. Life is not meant to be lived as a trap, because the way out or around a circumstance is always there, wide open and available, waiting for you to realize it. It's just that if you think your acts done out of compulsive thinking are all real, then life circumstances can feel like a trap. Whatever you think, feel, and do is your act. Whenever you fail to realize that, you think it's God's punishment, curses, or burdens when in reality actions are stemmed from the way you reacted. Your reaction was done compulsively which is unconsciously when you could have given it some thought and made it objectively, which is the alternative conscious way to respond.

You don't have to learn how to react, that happens automatically. You may, however, want to learn how to response more purposely in the way you would give advice to someone you love or hold dearly. The idea of reacting is acting how you may have acted in a similar but past situation. In a way that's almost done without thought. Like how someone sneaks up behind you and makes a loud noise, and you react. Or when someone says something to you in the same way they have, or someone else has in the past, and you reacted to it. The thing is, reacting is done without thinking. However, when that reaction is about keeping yourself safe like when someone is driving recklessly in your direction, or if someone is running at you with a gun, then reacting is a wonderful thing. That's distinctively different, because that's the part in your brain we discussed in chapter 15 designed to keep you alive and kicking in to survival mode.

Notice how those situations are truly dangerous, but how likely are you in your day-to-day operation of life approached with situations such as these that are physically dangerous? It's the not so physically dangerous times that you need to know how to respond. With respect to those who still participate in a particular lifestyle, a situation in which you are being approached by someone with a gun, you need to know how to respond as well as how to react. It could mean the difference between you walking away from that situation or not. I personally have had guns pointed at my head in three different occurrences in which the barrel of the gun actually touched my head on two of the occasions. I'd like to think my reaction as well as my response during these encounters is the reason I'm still alive. So I just want to voice that, because there is that little gray area for certain circumstances. So when you are indeed in danger, reacting with a touch of responding may be necessary. But notice how none of the situations you find yourself in on the day-to-day basis are truly dangerous. They may be a little unpleasant or things you may not be so crazy about, but they're not physically dangerous. It's in these situations you want to learn how to respond.

Again reacting is to re-act in a way you have in the past, but responding has the word sponsor as its core. What concept or thoughts do you want to sponsor? What emotion do you want to sponsor in others? What are you generally trying to accomplish in the situation? That has a more purposeful way of doing and being. If you're willing to respond in ways you would also recommend to someone you love, a way that's coinciding with your highest purpose, a way that defines how you want to be defined, then that response can go a long way toward creating the life you want. In that way you can become more influential in your life and the life of others. It'll have you thinking about how you want to say things before you actually say them.

Preparing a response to a situation and preparing a space between the things that happened in the past and how you choose to respond or create new actions is incredibly important, yet totally up to you. However, I'd like to go on record and acknowledge that this is a process, it doesn't happen overnight. I'm going to take the liberty in making some suggestion on how you can start the process of responding instead of reacting. The first step that I'll suggest would be to pause and take a second to reflect on the issue, even if just for a second. I'll admit it's easier said than done in a society where everything is continuously moving at a rapid pace. But sometimes taking a second to process your thoughts and choosing not to immediately assert your attention to the issue can be the best move for you in particular situations. The second thing you can do is to practice objective observation. Separating yourself and beginning to practice acknowledging what's actually happening. This is the course on not reacting to what you painted in your head about a particular person or situation, but actually looking at it for what is. It's kind of like having an outer body experience and stepping outside of yourself to visualize the situation from how you look playing a part and how your actions would be viewed by others. Another step I would suggest is paying attention to your own breathing. When something happens that you don't agree with or it may strike a nerve, pay attention to how your body language may react or change because of it. Notice how at this present moment that particular person or the situation at hand has more control over you than you do yourself. Notice how you lose control over your speech when you can't get your words to come out right, your body temperature when you start sweating, and your mentality when you're in a state of rage and you can't even think logically. Take the time to just breathe. Chances are, you're emotionally activated and that's not going to go away. So paying attention to your reactions will give you a focal point to aim your aggression in a healthier way. This allows you to focus on something different and not feed into the BS of how you once

211

would have reacted or who you once may have been, and give you some time instead to regulate your responses. Reflect on that change in your body and ask yourself if you really want to give someone or something else that much control of your physical well-being. I sure would hope not. There are plenty of people who are facing the rest of their life in a prison, or losing out on great positions in life by acting out in rage in the course of a split second decision. The final step is to forgive yourself when you go back to these old familiar ways of reacting (because you're human), and take a second to reflect, gather yourself, and understand by acknowledging how you went wrong, forgive yourself, and move forward.

Like I said earlier this is a process, and I spent a lot of time knowing and understanding the differences and steps to use as tools to keep me conscious of reacting and responding, and appreciating the fruits from doing so. It took a while before I was able to access and consistently utilize methods to control rage and, don't get me wrong, there are still those moments where I still have to apply them. This is about exerting these tools to create that space that allows you to access greatness from responding for a new outcome verses reacting and receiving what you may be used to. If I can prevent anyone from encountering any of my experiences or subjecting themselves to missing out on a blessing due to a lesson, it's all the more worth it to help someone help themself.

CHAPTER 21

Knowledge of Intellectual and Emotional Understanding

*"If a hundred-foot palm tree had the mind of a human,
it would only grow to be 6 feet tall."*
—T. Harv Eker

I purposely wanted to make this book 21 chapters. So I sat with my laptop thinking about what other major points I wanted to deliver or express in making you the greatest you. What I came up with is the difference between intellectual and emotional understanding. Understanding intellectually and understanding emotionally sound simple enough, right? But many of us fail to realize how most if not all of our decisions in life are made out of intelligence or emotions and how if we were keen to that knowledge, understanding that process can and would make for a better course in our lives. Let's say you gave yourself the challenge of trying to lose some weight. The intellectual part of it would be to stop eating carbs and exercise. The problems is whenever you get that bad news of the day and vent with that bottle of alcohol or vent with that box brownies and carton of ice cream, your understanding becomes emotional. Now that's the base of intellectual and emotional understanding.

When you face an obstacle or avoid a situation, are you doing it out of emotion or intelligence? Knowing your own mind can be simple once you become honest with yourself, but understanding it can be rather difficult. It can be hard to secure basic insights into your character or motivations. You may come to understand that there is a difference to observe between the knowing about yourself intellectually and knowing about yourself emotionally.

Nicole works a job as an architect. During a company meeting she presented some sketches from a couple of ideas she had pertaining to the development of some corporate office skyscrapers. Her boss laughed at her design, insulted her about her drawings, and told her that her ideas for such project would never appeal to anyone with class and taste. Confident enough in her work, she pursued her ideas and found funding for the project from another department. As a result, she got the building designed and constructed. When the praise and good press of such a beautiful building got back to the credit of the company, the owner was ecstatic, extremely impressed, and overwhelmed in joy with her work. However, the owner found out that she had to get funding from a completely different department and the reasons why. In his own way of complimenting her talent, he promoted Nicole and, to this day, the former boss who made a mockery of her work now asks her if the coffee he delivers is suitable.

Phillip was a professional basketball player with a promising career. After landing wrong while performing a dunk, he suffered an injury to his ankle which ultimately ended his career. Instead of sulking about the problem, he joined some on-line real estate courses while in the hospital and throughout his physical therapy. Since then he sold hundreds of properties and even designed a real-estate course himself, enabling him to become a multimillionaire.

Wanda got caught up and was falsely arrested for charges stemming from her (at the time) boyfriend's drug ring. Rather than stress and place blame on him and his actions, she instead passed the days of that time by composing books. She went from being a convicted felon to a New York Times best-selling author with over 25 books published, and she is now living her dream.

The moral of these stories is that if these individuals would have dwelled in their emotional understanding, they never would have been able to reap the benefits of their intellectual understanding.

You may not realize it, but emotional understanding is stronger than intellectual understanding. However, just as any habit can be created so can the habit of understanding intellectually as opposed to emotionally through a series of changes. I like to think of it as steps of transformation, because it's not enough to only change. Transformation is learning something that can produce results without thinking. The first step would be unconscious incompetence, and that is simply understanding that you don't know what you don't know. This can be a good place to start, because every day problems are in your head and that is not a good or healthy way to live. But if the results are not the way you want to be, then you should take a step back and look at them. You might then think that the reason for your current situation or problems are this, that, or whatever they may be. That's expected because the deeper you get into this way of thinking the closer you're moving to the next step, which is conscious incompetence. That's when you come to realize that there is this part of influence that you have. That's when you come to know that you can do something that you may have to learn but, ultimately, you then believe you can make a change in your situation. It's important to go from step one to two, and then to make a decision to say, "Ok, I'm going to learn something. I'm going to do something to change something, or at least try." That's the sign of you acknowledging the next phase, which is unconscious competence. This now becomes a really critical point, because you're now entering the third step and if you get lost there, you won't make the change. Why, you ask? Just think of the first time you learned how to ride a bike and how complicated it was. Think now how easy it became. Think about the first time you drove a car and how difficult it was. Now you can drive effortlessly because you've practiced continuously. You learned all of what was needed to learn until you reached the final step in this process of transformation, which is unconscious competence. You now can produce the results without thinking. This becomes the brilliant part, producing the results you want in your life without thinking anything or feeling anything.

Personal development is understood differently. The way I view it is being able to get more done in a less time. I've come to understand it's all about getting more done and maximizing results in one hour, it's not about working more hours. That's a major mistake people are tending to make. Your intensity has to step up, it's about the quality of time not the quantity. Tell yourself at the start of your day what you expect to accomplish, what goals are needed to be met before the end of the day, and what must be achieved to succeed in that outcome. I spoke earlier on the importance of being a good follower to enable you to be a great leader, but the simple fact is that we are all leaders because everyone leads themselves. After you have led yourself to a certain area you can lead others along with you. If you haven't reached this area, it would be impossible to successfully teach that to others. Therefore it's pertinent to understand how to lead yourself, and you do that through personal development. You should be open and honest enough to ask yourself, "How do I let myself be led?" and you do so by allowing yourself to be a good follower. By allowing yourself to be led means you give competence all the power you have. Not your ego and not you thinking you are right, because you're an expert. Find out where

216

the biggest competence is and that's where you need to dedicate your focus. It's there that you will be able to go from being the leader to being able to follow, and switch accordingly pertaining to your best interest. Understand the transformation from understanding intellectually and understanding emotionally is a process, and processes require an investment of time and energy. Grow your intensity of time. Be diligent and more proactive with the use of your time.

Something else that's very important in supporting where you're going with the process of intellectual and emotional understanding is comprehending the difference between knowing the work and doing the work. When I ask people what they should do or how people should perform, or the topic of the conversation is how children should be raised, they all come up with brilliant answers of what should be done, but their results are poor. That's because the intellectual understanding is on a high level, yet the emotional understanding is on a low level. As I thought over this I asked myself, "Why is it that way?" Maybe because people think that if they understood it intellectually they are strong and that's all that is required. But you only really understand something when you can produce the results without thinking and it can be done again, and again, not if you can tell other people how it should be done. This mistake is made time and time again. You may even know someone who fits this description; it may be even you, perhaps. The point is, if you really want to do something that's going to produce some results, you have to know where your place in life is. Now, for instance, people ask themselves, "What do I want to do?" Don't get me wrong, that's a good question but the better question is, "What am I meant for in life?" If you know that then you know where your place is in life, and you grow stronger as you excel in your

217

personal growth and/or career. You always notice your strengths because of the outcomes you produce, nothing else. Not the talking, not the wishing, and not even the great advice you have for others—it's your outcome. The outcome is everything you should steer your focus toward.

One of the most important lessons you will ever learn is that your mind is the greatest script writer in history. It makes up incredible stories, usually based on ambition and exaggerations that may never happen. It's important to understand that you are not your mind. You are much bigger and greater than your mind alone. Just as your hand or feet are a part of you, so is your mind. If a 100-foot palm tree had the mind of a human, it would only grow to be 6-feet tall. The worst thing you can do is to put a cap, margin, or height on your abilities. You must think and be limitless. Don't focus on your problems, focus on your goals. At the end of the day, you're either doing one of two things and that's thinking about the problems or focusing on the solutions. Successful people are solution-oriented. They used their time and energy strategizing and planning answers to challenges they may foresee, whether in the near or distant future, and then they create systems to prevent that problem from presenting itself again. Unsuccessful people are problem-oriented. They spend their time complaining and seldom come up with anything creative to alleviate the problem to make sure it doesn't happen again. Become a warrior in the definition of someone who conquers oneself. Don't back away from your problems nor should you avoid problems, but rather face them head on and knock them out of your way as if they were a measly fly annoying you. Bottom line is, you can become a master in handling problems and overcoming any obstacle. What can stop you from reaching success? The answer would have to be nothing and when nothing can stop you, then you become unstoppable. When you become unstoppable, then the question becomes what choices or options do you have in your life? The answers would be all choices and every option. If you are unstoppable anything and everything is available to you.

POSTFACE

Congratulations, greatness! Let me take the time out to salute you as we applaud and raise a toast to you and your accomplishing the study and actions along the course of becoming "The Greatest You." You've read attentively and diligently, and for all of your efforts may your rewards come in abundance. I can only hope that this book has taught you something and that you know more now than you knew before opening the first page.

We should all strive to become something greater in life and, once that goal is met and there's more life in you, continue to reach for more—if not for you then for your family, your culture, your legacy, or for generations to come. We should all aspire for something that adheres to our being of existence, and contribute to this world in a way that says you were here. Since it's a well-known fact and openly inevitable that every living soul will die, in this one chance at life how much of it do you want to live? Since it is your life, shouldn't that decision ultimately be left up to you? Shouldn't it be on your terms and by your standards? Where you are now is just a step toward where you are going. You control the wheel of your destination, it's just a matter of adjusting your GPS system and arriving there. Obstacles will present themselves, but they're just merely pit stops (like stopping for gas) toward your destination.

Being the greatest you starts with you wanting to be greater, and the steps in the course of this book is the means to help you do so. But the problem is so many people are afraid of change and, as a consequence, remain in an unlocked mind state, ignorant of the possibilities that may be presented. When we educate ourselves, we go through a process of opening up mentally as we are allowing our minds to unlock and remove old behaviors and re-lock and receive new information to establish new behaviors. When we are adhering to new learning our minds go through the process of re-locking in what's being understood. It's important to understand that I didn't write this book for my readers to have a quick read through, been there done that, one and done type of experience. That merely entertains you as a typical novel would. I wrote this book to be a study guide to life and all throughout your life. The chapters will appeal to different times of difficulties and troubles you may face. I composed it in this way mainly due to the omnipresence of life's many challenges, circumstances, and situations that have more twists and turns than a Rubik's cube and unforeseeable problems we all encounter.

Don't make your journey in life harder than what it has to be. Concentrate on what's there and not on what may or could be. Give things your own interpretation. Ask yourself what do (or can) others benefit from of your existence. Don't think about what you can't control. Understand that you lead you, and put full trust into that burning desire of that vision you have. Encourage yourself with the challenge for more. Develop a hunger for knowledge. Seek the required necessities to position yourself in the life you want to be living today, tomorrow, and for the rest of your journey. I want you to exceed excellence, I want you to reach for it because you can, because it's there for you in the world to reach, and it's there for you to grab onto and possess. It's here for you in this world to obtain, to improve, and to re-create for the betterment of your society and our entire world. It's your course in life and those that follow behind your genetic footsteps.

The beauty about success is that you earn it. It cannot be handed down like a business or wealth. You can will yourself

221

to become anything that you set out to be in life. The challenge is, are you going to remain true to who you are when faced with adversity? Never give up on yourself, continue to shine even through darkness, because that's where true stars are born when situations look hopeless. Always keep in mind that what you wake up with on Thursday is because of the work you put in Wednesday, Tuesday, Monday, and so on. What you physically possess today is because of the decisions you made yesterday. No one puts in the work but you, and keep in mind that who you are now is a direct result of who you have been. Understand you have the power to make this life exactly what and how you want it. By no means should you have to settle and by no means should you accept. It all stems from decision-making and choices. Yet your choices and decisions stem from knowledge, experiences, perseverance, dedication, and ambition. It comes from all the qualities I want you to develop that are expressed throughout this book. Those are qualities that are already in you, that you must find from within, and failure is not an option. No matter how bad it is or how bad it gets, you are going to make it. Giving up is never an option. Perseverance of abundance is what I want for you until the last day of your life—dream it, obtain it, and claim it. You think it, you strive for it, and you get it. Anything less is unacceptable. Thank you!

$ Be The Greatest You $

ABOUT THE AUTHOR

Mister Williams is an aspiring entrepreneur who is the founder and C.E.O. of Ball Out Family Entertainment and All Ball Out Publications. He is a Bay Area-based California resident who has always had the art for storytelling and picked up the passion for composing books of his own since 2008. Writing is the best outlet for him to combine his love, fascination, and knowledge of philosophy and psychology. It is his goal for his readers to experience the full immersion of the many realities of this world through a plethora of literature.